VINTAGE AIRCRAFT
OVER AMERICA

VINTAGE AIRCRAFT
OVER
AMERICA

Geoff Jones
& Chuck Stewart

Airlife

Acknowledgements

Thanks to all who have made their beautiful and historically important aircraft available to the authors and flown them so expertly for the camera. Many of the air-to-air shoots were executed from a Cessna 172 camera plane in Californian skies. A Cessna 150 and Piper PA-34 Seneca were also used, and for one shoot a DHC-1 Chipmunk. Particular thanks are also due to Delta Air Lines.

Half Title page
Ryan PT-20 (1940)
A neatly cowled inline 125 hp Menasco C4 engine powers Dan Mairani's Ryan PT-20, although many of the marque delivered to the USAAC were fitted with Kinner radials *(GPJ)*

Title page
North American Navion/Navion Rangemaster H (1946)
Doug Hoogeveen flies his 1947 North American Navion clear of some stormy weather off the Californian coast *(CRS)*

Copyright © 2002 Geoff Jones and Chuck Stewart

First published in the UK in 2002 by Airlife Publishing Ltd

British Library Cataloguing-in-Publication Data
   A catalogue record for this book
   is available from the British Library

ISBN 1 84037 296 6

Typeset by Rowland Phototypesetting Limited, Bury St Edmunds, Suffolk
Printed in Hong Kong.

For a complete list of all Airlife titles please contact:

Airlife Publishing Ltd
101 Longden Road, Shrewsbury, SY3 9EB, England
E-mail: sales@airlifebooks.com
Website: www.airlifebooks.com

This is a journey through time and through the lens, looking at some of the most evocative civil and general aviation aircraft that have been designed in the United States and which are still, in many cases, gracing American and European skies. A primary criterion for inclusion here is that they are airworthy, or have been long after they were built. Most have been photographed, air-to-air, and in a few instances ground-to-air. They are a tribute to their owners and restorers who are preserving aeronautical heritage in its very best aspect – in the air.

Most of the aircraft featured were photographed between 1998 and 2001. Some shots have emerged from the depths of our libraries and date back to the 1980s, including those of Bill Rose's lovely Grumman Goose, although the aircraft itself was seen flying in Florida in 2000. The late Jim Nissen's Curtiss Jenny is now grounded, but preserved for posterity in a museum at Ogden, Utah.

Thirty-seven different types are featured, in several cases with more than one example. Size is immaterial, and they range from the diminutive, homebuilt Pietenpol Aircamper to the grandeur of the world's ultimate propeller-powered airliner, the Lockheed Constellation.

This is a sequel to our first volume for Airlife Publishing Ltd published in January 2000, *American Classics of the Air*.

Geoff Jones and Chuck Stewart

Contents

The date in brackets is that of the first recorded flight of each prototype, although the first flight date of many of the actual examples featured is different.

Introduction

The output of American aircraft companies during the twentieth century was prolific. Fuelled by the post-First World War boom in technology, the emergence of innumerable small manufacturers, and the effects of the second world war, the variety, shape, purpose and handling of their products was highly varied. Depicted in this book are many well-known types such as the Piper J-3 Cub, of which more than 20 000 were built, and the Douglas DC-3, which had a production run in the U.S.A. of 10 926 in all its variants. Most of the aircraft featured first flew in the hey-day of the American industry in the 1930s and 1940s, although the Curtiss Jenny pre-dates this. There are also a few *new* classics from the 1950s to the 1980s. Less well-known types such as the Harlow PJC-2, of which only twelve were built, are also featured.

This book, as with *American Classics of the Air*, our first and similar work, concentrates largely on the output of the civil aircraft manufacturers. Beech, Cessna, Ryan, Stinson, Aeronca and several other 1930s companies whose forte was civilian aircraft, shifted with the demand for wartime production into the military sector, albeit producing variants of their successful civilian models. However, all the aircraft featured are now civilian, operated by civilian owners and on their respective countries' civilian registers. Larger airliner types such as the Douglas DC-3, Martin 404 and Lockheed Constellation are also worthy types amongst their smaller brethren in this book.

Several of these American classics are Europe-based. The trade in aircraft across the Atlantic has been immense, particularly to the UK and vice versa. This has been to the unquestionable benefit of pilots, collectors and enthusiasts around the world. While many of the aircraft pictured will make you long to be able to gaze up at American skies, there are many Americans who are equally envious of the depth, variety and activity of the antique and classic aircraft arenas in the UK, and, to a lesser extent, other parts of Europe. By 2000, France was becoming a home for a fascinating variety of American classics, largely imported from the U.S.A.

The oldest type featured here is the famous Curtiss Jenny, the big American aircraft success of the First World War, with 10 900 built both in the U.S.A. and Canada. Among the most modern are the Navion Rangemaster H and Cessna A185F Skywagon. Although the Navion Rangemaster featured was built as recently as 1970, its design lineage can be traced back to the North American NA-145 Navion which first flew in April 1946. Its inclusion is therefore fully justified. Similarly the Cessna 185, a strengthened and enlarged version of the Cessna 180 whose prototype first flew in May 1952.

The most evocative era has to be the 1930s with its classic biplanes such as the Waco and Beech Staggerwing. However, the decade was also the dawn of the first truly successful commercial air transports, notably the Douglas DC-3. The one we have chosen is probably the most pristine of its kind now flying, a tribute to Delta Air Lines whose support and backing has enabled a dedicated Atlanta team to restore one of the airline's original aircraft to a condition undoubtedly better than when it was first delivered in December 1940.

Another classic type here is the Pietenpol Aircamper. This is the only home-built type featured, but, along with the French Mignet HM-14 Pou-du-Ciel (Flying Flea) and the Heath Parasol, it probably contributed more to the amateur-build aircraft movement than any other. World-renowned sport aircraft associations such as the Experimental Aircraft Association (EAA), the Popular Flying Association (PFA) of the UK, and the Réseau du Sport de l'Air (RSA) of France probably owe a huge debt of gratitude to pioneer amateur builders such as Bernie Pietenpol.

Curtiss JN-4D 'Jenny' (1916)

The Jenny is probably one of the best-known aeroplanes ever built. It is the one that got America into aviation and was the one the barnstormers and early wing-walkers used. It actually originated in Britain where B. Douglas Thomas of the Sopwith Aeroplane Company drew up a design known as the Type J to a Curtiss specification. Blended in the U.S.A. with Curtiss's Type N specification, it was designated as the JN-2. From these two letters the nickname 'Jenny' was created – and stuck through generations.

Only a few of the JN-2 were built, including ten for the United States Army. An improved JN-3 followed and subsequently in 1916 the ubiquitous JN-4. It differed from the earlier models by having a single stick control for elevators and ailerons – the JN-2 and JN-3 used the Deperdussin method of control with separate controls for the rudder, elevators and ailerons.

Another landmark feature of the Jenny was its engine, the 90 hp Curtiss OX-5 inline. Most contemporary engines were rotary. The inline OX-5 was more reliable, more efficient and became the standard fit for American-designed and built aircraft for much of the 1920s and even into the early 1930s. It was arguably the most significant engine in early American aviation. However, on the orders of the US Air Corps in 1927 all surviving Jenny aircraft and

Jenny airframe parts were to be destroyed, a decision intended to stop the escapades of barnstormers around the United States!

The Curtiss JN-4D Jenny pictured was photographed at Watsonville, California, in 1985 and 1990. It was owned, restored and flown by Jim Nissen from Livermore in California. It was originally built in 1918 and is claimed to be 90% original. Nissen found the aircraft in 1957 near Portland, Oregon, on a farm owned by Mrs Leo Elwert. He bought it with his partner James Mathiesen, and when Mathiesen died, Nissen bought his share. It was then moved to Livermore for the rebuild. The restoration of the OX-5 engine was carried out by the late Fred Wagner who once ran a workshop at Oakland airport.

New parts for the Jenny either had to be made from scratch or traded among other Jenny owners, most of whom used their aircraft only for static displays at the time of Nissen's restoration. The propeller had to be hand-carved from scratch and there was no known source of tyres. The Jenny was first flown again after a rebuild lasting nearly five years in April 1976 and made its public debut a month later at the Watsonville Antique Fly-In organised by the Northern California Antique Airplane Association. It was the undisputed 'Grand Champion'. Nissen died in April 1994 and

OPPOSITE PAGE:
This unique British-based Great Lakes biplane is owned and flown by Robert Fray *(GPJ)*

Slowly but surely Jim Nissen coaxes his restored Curtiss Jenny through the Californian skies at the Watsonville Fly-In in May 1990, 72 years after it was built *(GPJ)*

it took his family a few years to find a suitable home for the aircraft. In late 1999 it was donated to the Air Force Aerospace Museum at Ogden, Utah, where it is preserved in non-airworthy condition, still with civil registration N5001.

Europe's only genuine Jenny is owned by Vic Norman in the UK and was kept at Rendcomb airfield near Cirencester. Built in 1917, it was civil-registered in the U.S.A. as N2525 before becoming G-ECAB in the UK in 1999. It was expected to be moved from Rendcomb to the Shuttleworth Trust's new hangar during 2001. Several Jenny replicas still fly occasionally and others are kept in non-airworthy condition in museums.

The first JN aircraft were delivered to the US Army's Signal Corps in 1916 and some saw active service on the Mexican border with Pershing, one of America's greatest soldiers. The Curtiss company built approximately 10 900, including 2900 in Canada. The US Army Air Service procured 6163 from 1917 to 1918. Some 95% of all American and Canadian pilots took their initial flight training during the first world war in the Jenny. At the end of the war several thousand of the aircraft were sold as surplus and many were used in barnstormers and other air show acts. Many Americans took their first flights or flips in a Curtiss Jenny at country fairs and flying demonstrations, before the 1927 Air Corps decision.

Nissen's flying career started when he was 14 when he designed, built and flew – or rather, hopped – his own glider in the countryside east of San Francisco. His first proper solo was in an Aeronca C-2. He flew the PBY for the United States Navy between San Diego and Hawaii, Boeing and Martin flying-boats for Pan American Airways, and concluded his professional flying career as a research test pilot for Naca (the National Advisory Committee for Aeronautics, forerunner of Nasa), spending some of his time at the Ames research facility at Sunnyvale. He leased some land in 1946 near San Jose, created a small airport and, after the city became interested in it, he was appointed manager, a post he held for 27 years. He had to retire to have the time to work on his Jenny, starting in the autumn of 1971, and flying it for more than 500 hours between 1976 and 1990. The beautiful aircraft he saved and preserved is finished in the colours of the United States Army Air Service, based at Love Field, Dallas, Texas.

As well as a 90% original airframe, the redoubtable 90 hp Curtiss OX-5 engine's restoration was a remarkable achievement in itself, the work of the late Fred Wagner *(GPJ)*

Brunner-Winkle Bird A and BK (1928)

It was Mr A. Brunner, secretary and partial financial backer, and William E. Winkle, vice-president, who provided the rather bizarre aircraft company name. Michael Gregor, a Russian refugee, was the Brunner-Winkle Aircraft Corporation designer, as well as its chief engineer.

Development of the Bird A was partly due to the availability of a good number of war-surplus OX-5 engines. This type was entered in the 1929 Guggenheim Safe Airplane Contest, its short take-off, 120 mph top speed and safe handling at only 40 mph helping it to score the highest marks for conventional aircraft.

The red Bird A pictured (N14K) is the one in which Melba Beard won the women pilots' trophy at the 1935 National Air Races at Cleveland, Ohio, with the coveted prize presented by Amelia Earhart. Ownership passed to Melba's daughter Arlene, who continued to fly the aircraft in California well into the 1990s. Although a plaque placed in front of the aircraft at air shows claims that it dates from 1928, this is unlikely for this particular one. The prototype Bird A first flew in September 1928, and was used for extensive test flying and promotion work. Production by the company didn't begin at its Glendale facility at Brooklyn, New York, until 1929. This Bird A has a Kinner engine, which must have been fitted later in its life.

The distinctive Bird BK (NC847W) was owned by Amelia and Robin Reid, and based at Reid-Hillview airport at San Jose, California, when photographed in May 1990. Amelia Reid, an accomplished pilot who learnt to fly in the 1950s, opened a flying school at Reid-Hillview in 1960. She also flew airshow routines in a variety of aircraft from 1966 onwards. She died in March 2001.

This aircraft is powered by a five-cylinder, air-cooled 100 hp Kinner K-5 engine. When availability of the OX-5 engine, the mainstay of power for small aircraft since the first world war, became doubtful, Brunner-Winkle decided in October 1929 to substitute the new Kinner K-5 engine. This determined the aircraft's designation – it was the model B with a Kinner engine, hence Bird BK. The type earned its place in aviation history when Colonel Charles Lindbergh bought one for his wife, Anne, and in it she completed flying training in 1930 to obtain her pilot's licence.

Both the Bird A and the early BK were three-seaters, with side-by-side seating for two in the front cockpit and the pilot sitting behind. Most notable, though, was the sesquiplane arrangement of the wings, the thick-section, upper wing representing nearly 70% of the lifting area. Later variants of the Bird BK were fitted with different engines, the Bird BW with a 125 hp Warner, and the Bird CJ and CK – with a 170 hp Jacobs; the CK had room for three in the front cockpit. As with many aircraft manufacturers in the early 1930s, the Depression took its toll and the factory closed in 1932 after 130 of the Bird B and C had been built.

Amelia and Robin Reid arrive at the Watsonville Fly-In on California's west coast from their home base at Reid-Hillview airport near San Jose. NC847W was built in 1929 *(GPJ)*

▲
Still a stunner decades after it was built, this Bird A was taken over by Melba Beard's daughter, Arlene, when Melba died. The Birds seem to have been popular with women pilots. Amelia Reid flies the other example shown here, while Anne Morrow Lindbergh, Charles Lindbergh's wife, learnt to fly in one in 1930 *(GPJ)*

▶

A five-cylinder, air-cooled, 100 hp Kinner K-5 powers this Bird A. This engine was widely used in the late 1920s and 1930s for a variety of civil aircraft types *(GPJ)*

Command Aire (1928)

The featured aircraft is, in fact, a Command Aire 5C3 (NC997E). By 1994, when most of these photos were taken, it had clocked up more than 130 hours' flight time after a lengthy rebuild by Bob Lock. Lock bought the remains of the aircraft in 1978; after most of the restoration had been completed he displayed the aircraft in static form at the Sun 'n Fun Air Museum at Lakeland, Florida. It was then brought up to airworthy condition and flown across the U.S.A. to its new home in Reedley, California, where Lock runs his aircraft restoration company, Aero Lock. Bob's son, Robert, a former professional basketball player, is also an aviation enthusiast, between them they have restored not only the Command Aire but several Stearman too and a New Standard D-25 (NC9756) that was based at Powell, Ohio.

Restoration of the Command Aire involved Lock in discussions with the aircraft's designer, Albert Vollmecke, who, despite his age, visited Lock's workshop to supervise manufacture of replacement parts, give advice on rigging, and provide many other helpful tips. Vollmecke had been employed in Germany by Ernst Heinkel. In 1927 he joined the Arkansas Aircraft Co., which had been founded the previous year to engage in commercial flying, as its chief engineer.

The first Command Aire was the 3C3, brought out by the Arkansas company at Little Rock in about January 1928. This three-seater had the venerable 90 hp Curtiss OX-5 engine. A succession of Command Aire designs were built in the late 1920s, each with different engines:

Model	Engine	
3C3	(Curtiss OX-5)	Three-seater
3C3-A	(Warner 110)	Three-seater
3C3-B, 4C3	(Siemens-Halske)	Three-seater
3C3-T	(Curtiss OX-5)	Two-seater
3C3-AT	(Warner 110)	Two-seater
5C3	(Curtis Challenger 170)	Three-seater
5C3-A	(Hispano-Suiza 150)	Three-seater
3C3-BT	(Siemens-Halske)	Two-seater
5C3-B	(Axelson 115-150)	Three-seater
5C3-C	(Wright J6-5-165)	Three-seater

The most popular Command Aire models built, apart from the OX-5 versions, were the Warner 110 and Curtiss Challenger-powered models. In all, more than 200 Command Aires were built, and many were used as trainers. During the latter stages of production a new Command Aire, with a 165 hp Wright J6 engine, sold for $6025. Production slowed during 1930 and the company went out of business in 1931.

Only two Command Aires were known to be airworthy and flying in 2001. Lock's aircraft, although a 5C3, is fitted with the 110 hp Warner radial engine. It cruises at 95 mph, stalls at 46 mph, and consumes 12 US gallons of fuel per hour in the cruise.

◀ The non-standard engine in Bob Lock's Command Aire 5C3 is a 110 hp Warner radial with metal Hamilton Standard propeller *(CRS)*

▲ Over the vast tracts of farmland of California's Central Valley, Bob Lock flies his unique 1929 Command Aire 5C3 *(GPJ)*

Great Lakes Biplane (1929)

Charles 'Charlie' W. Meyer, former first world war pilot, Waco employee and later an Eastern Air Lines captain, combined his knowledge and talents with Boeing designer Cliff Liesey in the U.S.A. in 1928 to design a pilot's aeroplane. Based in some workshops on the shores of Lake Erie, the aircraft, a tandem, two-seat biplane, was named the Great Lakes Sport Trainer. Making its debut in March 1929 at the Detroit Air Show, it was well received, and the newly-formed Great Lakes Aircraft Corporation (GLAC) established a production line in the former Glen L. Martin factory at Cleveland, Ohio.

Initial production was of the 2-T-1 with an inline, air-cooled 85 hp Cirrus Mk 3 engine, a licence-built version of the British four-cylinder inline engine. Next followed the Great Lakes 2-T-1A Sport, with a 100 hp Cirrus and by mid-1929 GLAC reputedly had a backlog of orders for 200 aircraft. With air racing success already to its name, further publicity for the type was ensured with the legendary 'Tex' Rankin's August 1929 non-stop three-flags flight in a Great Lakes 2-T-1 from Canada, over the U.S.A. to Mexico. In January 1930 Rankin established a new world record in a Great Lakes, completing nineteen consecutive outside loops.

By this time every sport pilot wanted to fly or own a Great Lakes biplane; GLAC had 750 staff and the order book had swelled to 700 aircraft. However, the stock market crash shattered the dreams of many would-be owners. The ex-works price of a Great Lakes biplane in 1930 was $4990; by 1931 this had been drastically reduced to $2985 to try to stimulate demand. By mid-1932 a total of 264 had been built, including the new 2-T-1E with a 95 hp Cirrus Hi-Drive engine. The writing was on the wall, though. By 1933 the once grand GLAC had faded into oblivion.

Featured here is one of the 100 hp Cirrus-engined Great Lakes that came off the Cleveland production line in 1932. It is a rare survivor from the era, and one of the remaining few outside the U.S.A.

Its restorer and owner is UK-based Robert Fray, a 57-year-old farmer. The aircraft had been found derelict in an Ohio barn in the late 1980s. It was shipped to England and in 1989 Fray bought the remains. The biggest decision during the restoration was what engine to fit. Fray didn't have access to a Cirrus, didn't want to fit a Lycoming radial, and thought about a Warner Scarab from a Stearman but discovered it would be too heavy. Eventually he came across a picture in a magazine of a Great Lakes biplane at Oshkosh. It had a Kinner engine, with characteristic cylinder heads protruding from an otherwise smooth and pointed nose. He liked the look of this, verified that such an engine fit was historically authentic and that it was within the weight limitations for the type. He acquired a Gladden Kinner R55 engine, and this is what is now fitted.

The aircraft is c/n 126 and ex-NC865K; in November 1992 during the rebuild it was registered G-BUPV. The first post-restoration flight from Fray's base at Sibson, near Peterborough, was in May 1998 with pilot Barry Tempest. The aircraft has subsequently flown about 60 hours, most of it on local flights around eastern England. Fray enjoys the total contrast and challenge of flying this classic, and the relaxation it provides, pottering about at a modest 90 mph in the cruise with no radio and with the characteristic pop-pop noise of the Kinner engine for company. This valuable artefact was not rebuilt for aerobatic flight, so all Fray's flying is gentle turns and straight and level. It can still easily out-perform a Cessna 152 as we discovered climbing out of Sibson for the air-to-air photo shoot, looking for columns of sunlight beneath the fair-weather cumulus clouds of a typical English summer's day.

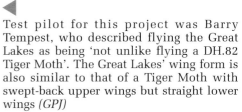

Test pilot for this project was Barry Tempest, who described flying the Great Lakes as being 'not unlike flying a DH.82 Tiger Moth'. The Great Lakes' wing form is also similar to that of a Tiger Moth with swept-back upper wings but straight lower wings *(GPJ)*

OPPOSITE PAGE:
A superb restoration of the 1932 Great Lakes biplane was carried out by Robert Fray in England between 1989 and 1998. The Gladden Kinner R55 engine, while not unique, is historically accurate but a rarity these days on restored Great Lakes biplanes *(GPJ)*

The vertical tail on later models of Great Lakes biplanes was enlarged. Several other significant design changes occurred during the type's main production run between 1929 and 1933 *(GPJ)*

Pietenpol Aircamper (1929)

No other aircraft, with the possible exception of the French Mignet HM 14 Pou-du-Ciel (Flying Flea), has had such a dramatic effect on the amateur-build movement as Bernard H. 'Bernie' Pietenpol's two-seat, tandem Aircamper from the late 1920s.

Pietenpol, a self-taught mechanic, was born in Spring Valley, Minnesota, in 1901. During the early 1920s he developed his first home-build biplane, the single-seat Sky Scout, credited with flying in 1923 powered by a converted Ford Model T automobile engine rated at 35 hp. Friends in Spring Valley reputedly asked Pietenpol: 'What about a monoplane?'

By April 1929 he had completed the design and construction of his prototype, a single-seat Aircamper with a parasol wing. As he didn't own a drill or a welding torch, everything was either bolted or riveted together. These were austere times, in a mainly rural and agricultural U.S.A. The Aircamper's construction was based around easily obtained and inexpensive components, the main structure being of wood from the local timber merchant. The blacksmith provided fabricated fittings; cotton covering came from discarded bed linen; clear varnish was used; the landing gear was constructed from second-hand gas pipes and wheels from a motorcycle. A hand-carved propeller of black walnut was fitted to a four-cylinder, water-cooled, Ace motorcycle engine. Pietenpol flew this single-seat prototype for more than 50 hours in two months.

Friends again made constructive comments to Pietenpol. A more powerful Ford Model A engine was adopted, and it was suggested that a two-seater would be more sociable. The fuselage was stretched and the wingspan increased, with a split-axle landing gear for better ground handling and rough-field operations. This prototype first flew in 1931.

Pietenpol shared his experiences of the two-seat Aircamper with the American public in 1934 through the pages of *Modern Mechanix* magazine and advertised complete sets of plans in

Flying and Glider Manual. The plans sold for $7.50, and he also started to sell basic kits of pre-cut wooden parts for $70. It was estimated that a customer could build an Aircamper for around $500. Copies of Pietenpol's original 1931 plans were still available in 2001 for $75 from Bernie's son, Don Pietenpol, who lives in Rochester, Minnesota.

It is impossible to say how many examples of the two-seat Aircamper have been completed and flown. Homebuilders all over the world have taken off in Aircampers, with the variety of engines used being exceeded only by the number of host countries. As well as the original Ford A and T, builders have fitted the Ford V-8, Kinner radial, Chevrolet Corvair, Lycoming and Continental.

The Pietenpol Aircamper featured here was built from the 1931 drawings, but like most of the type it has many idiosyncratic features. For instance, the Continental A-65-8 engine came from the wreckage of a 1941 Aeronca Chief. Construction started in 1974 with EAA 'Chapter 180' (a regional branch of EAA) at Sarasota in Florida. Build quality was good, but, as with many homebuilt projects, enthusiasm waned. Gene and Greg Utley then acquired the project and in 1990 enlisted the respected Florida builder Rick Berstling to help complete the aircraft. It flew for the first time in 1993, just a few weeks after Gene Utley's premature death. Since then it has been flown for more than 300 hours, many of them from Berstling's grass strip at Myakka City in Florida.

In 1999 there were celebrations of the life and work of Bernard Pietenpol – it was the 70th anniversary of the first flight of the prototype Aircamper. Pietenpol's vision was simple and practical enough to endure for decades. There are now probably more pilots than ever building and flying Aircampers. About 2500 hours should be allowed by anyone contemplating building one. It is well worth the effort; the finished product will be a practical, fun-to-fly machine that can safely carry two people on fair-weather jaunts.

◀ ▲

Bernard H. Pietenpol's 1929 design started as a single-seat, parasol-wing Aircamper. In 1931 he enlarged the design to a two-seater, ensuring its continued popularity ever since as a home-build design *(GPJ)*

OPPOSITE PAGE:
As Aircampers are built by amateurs at home, each example has its idiosyncrasies. This example has 2° dihedral on the wings – the 1931 plans show a completely straight wing. Rick Berstling believes this enhances its performance and looks *(GPJ)*

Monocoupe 90 (1930)

Inspired by the success of its 113, the Mono Aircraft Corporation of Moline, Illinois, introduced the Monocoupe 90 in 1930.

The tiny, side-by-side two seater quickly proved its mettle in air tours, derbies and races. In the gruelling 1930 National Air Tour, company pilot Bart Stevenson flew a model 90 to twelfth place, seizing the spotlight from perennial winner Bellanca.

Its performance in such well-publicised events helped make the Monocoupe 90 a big seller even as the American economy staggered through the Depression.

When it made its debut in 1930, the 90 sold for $3375. Despite good sales in 1931–32, when the Curtiss-Wright Airplane Co. (also based at Lambert Field in St Louis, where Mono Aircraft moved in late 1931) became the national distributor for Monocoupe, the price was cut to $2885 in 1933.

In 1934, when the American economy began showing signs of recovery, Monocoupe slicked up the basic 90 design, adding a tunnel-type engine cowling and a few other modifications and calling it the 90 Deluxe. Even with a sticker price of $3485, it was a success and led to the development of the 90A in 1935.

By mid-1934, nearly 1000 of the Monocoupe series had been sold, making it one of the predominant types on the American light aircraft scene. Although the glory years ended in 1940 when the company was dissolved and moved to Orlando, Florida, as a subsidiary of Universal Molded Products, the 90 design still had some life left in it.

After the second world war, the type certificate for the last of the series, the Monocoupe 90-AF and AL, was purchased by a Florida company and limited production continued from 1954 to 1957. Today, 118 Monocoupes of all types remain in the U.S.A.; 11 of them are model 90s and there are 51 of the model 90A.

The gorgeous yellow and black Monocoupe featured belongs to Carl Moore, a 69-year-old retired industrial photographer from

Elden Iler's 1935 Monocoupe 90A. The cockpit is a tight squeeze for two, but it cruises at 110-plus mph *(CRS)*

The Monocoupe 90A featured an overhead skylight built into the one-piece, 32 ft wing, as well as flaps and adjustable horizontal stabiliser *(CRS)*

Milpitas, California. It's a 1933 Model 90 that he bought in 1978 after a previous owner groundlooped it.

NC12361 passed through several owners who planned to restore it but never did, so when Moore acquired it, it was a basketcase. Restoring it took nearly two decades.

Moore rebuilt the fuselage in his garage, the wing in a rented hangar at Hollister Airport. The plane was red when he got it, but Moore painted it yellow and black because he liked the combination and thought it fitted with other colour schemes of the 1930s.

Seventeen years after he began, Moore made the first post-restoration flight in late 1995. It has been fun, uneventful flying ever since, said Moore of the aircraft that has won numerous 'Outstanding Golden Age Cabin Monoplane' trophies at fly-ins all over northern California.

Little is known of NC12361's early history. New, it served as a Monocoupe company hack and, according to Moore, may have been flown by Charles Lindbergh during a visit to St Louis.

In 1935, it was sold to a doctor in Kilgore, Texas. Just before the second world war, it was wrecked by a student on the civilian pilot training program in Texas.

NC12361 still has its original powerplant: a five-cylinder, 90 hp Lambert R-266 radial turning a Hamilton-Standard ground-adjustable metal propeller. The engine used to have an exhaust collector ring, but when it rusted, a previous owner hack-sawed it off, leaving short, noisy individual stacks.

At 2000 rpm, the 90 cruises at 95–100 mph and throws oil like mad.

Although the Monocoupe 90 was a success, very few changes had been made to the design during its first three years in production, and sales began to slow.

In the meantime, there was plenty of action in the company's boardroom. In late 1931, Mono Aircraft relocated to Lambert Field and changed its name to the Monocoupe Corporation.

Two years later, company founder Don Luscombe left for Kansas City to build the Phantom under his own name and was replaced as president by Wooster Lambert. By 1936, Lambert had been replaced and the prolific Al Mooney joined the company as chief designer.

When the economy began picking up in 1934, Monocoupe responded with its first major changes to the 90. The result was the 90 Deluxe.

It was followed by the 90A, which proved to be the most popular of the series, in 1935. One of its hallmarks was the 145 hp, seven-cylinder Warner radial, a major increase in power from the 90 hp Lambert, wrapped under a beautiful bumped Naca cowl.

The 90A had other features that were well ahead of their time: an overhead skylight built into the one-piece, 32-ft wing, flaps and an adjustable horizontal stabiliser.

The blue and white 1935 Monocoupe 90A featured here is owned by Elden Iler, a 50-year-old plastering contractor from Van Nuys, California. He bought it in 1966 from the Owl's Head Transportation Museum in Maine.

NC11782 was originally restored in 1971. But after being flown for five years, it was sent to veteran restorer Gar Williams of Naperville, Illinois, to be rebuilt again. This time, it got a new, scratch-built wing and new parts throughout.

It was then purchased by Tom Watson, former IBM chairman and a trustee of the Owl's Head Museum. In time, he donated it to the museum, and when the museum decided to sell it, Iler was the first of 30 people to call about it.

Iler put it on a trailer and towed it home to California where he reassembled it. After nearly 50 hours of flying, its 145 hp Warner Scarab radial blew a cylinder, grounding it for much of 2000.

A 90 hp engine gave the Monocoupe 90 a top speed of 115–118 mph *(CRS)*

The 90's simple plywood instrument panel is dominated by throttle and magneto switches in the centre *(CRS)*

Carl Moore designed the paint job on his 1933 Monocoupe to highlight its classic 1930s lines *(CRS)*

Beech 17 Staggerwing (1932)

A product of the genus that evolved from the Wichita, Kansas-based Travel Air Company, the first design from the Beech Aircraft Company was a stunning and eye-catching addition to the more run-of-the-mill aircraft that rival companies were building in the post-Depression years in America. Named the Staggerwing because of the negative stagger of the upper wings in relation to the lower, this innovative concept also had aerodynamic and structural advantages over rival biplanes at the time including the vastly improved forward and upward visibility from the cockpit.

The Travel Air Company had employed Walter Beech – as well as Clyde Cessna and Lloyd Stearman – but when Beech decided he needed a new challenge he teamed up with businessman K. K. Shaul and engineer Ted Wells to set up the Beech Aircraft Company in 1932. Wells had been working on several new designs before this, but the 420 hp Wright R-975-E2 radial-engined Beech 17 prototype (499N) was the pinnacle of his work.

The prototype first flew on 4 November 1932. The main differences from later models were the undercarriage (the wheels retracted only slightly into the fairings in flight), a different wing profile and a shorter fuselage.

Construction of all civilian Beech 17 Staggerwings was on an almost customised and individual basis. They were the Rolls-Royce of the air in the 1930s, bought by discerning and wealthy customers. In 1933 the factory price of the Beech 17-R was $19 000, but the following year this was reduced to $17 930. It was only in 1934 that significant numbers of the Beech 17 started to appear, when the B series was introduced with a choice of four different engines and a fully retractable landing gear. The most popular choice was the B17L with a 225 hp Jacobs L-4 radial engine. In 1936 the C17 was introduced and, in 1937, the D17 and E17. Mike Bell's beautiful aircraft, featured here, was built in the latter part of 1937, the 196th Staggerwing to come off Beech's Wichita production line.

A fully retractable undercarriage featured on all but the first few Staggerwings built in 1932–33 *(GPJ)*

Bell, an anaesthetist, acquired his E17B (N41663) in the late 1980s when he bought it from the Brennan family in California. Soon he had completed a major internal refit and re-upholstering of the aircraft's interior. Between 1998 and 2000 the aircraft was grounded while engine problems were sorted out, wing-rigging adjusted and other minor niggles addressed. When the accompanying photos were taken over the Californian mountains near Vacaville/Nut Tree in September 2000, Bell's Staggerwing had been back in the air for just two weeks and he was flying it at every available opportunity. During the Staggerwing's grounding, Mike had kept his hand in with radial-engined aircraft, buying first a North American AT-6 and then a Yak-18T.

Beech built a total of 781 model 17 biplanes between 1932 and 1948. When the world went to war, Beech adapted the Staggerwing for the US Army and Navy for light transport and communications duties. A total of 207 Staggerwings were built for the Army (UC-43), and 63 for the Navy (GB-2). A further 118 civilian models were known to have been pressed into military service. Thirty UC-43 models and 75 of the GB-2 were supplied to the Royal Navy under lend-lease arrangements, and known as the Traveller 1.

The final variant of the Staggerwing, the G.17S, was introduced after the war in 1946 at a list price of $29 000. Only fifteen were built between 1946 and 1947. Sales evaporated, because customers no longer wanted larger radial-engined biplanes. Beech sold the remaining parts to the Henry Seale Aviation Supply Co. of Dallas, Texas, which assembled the final four Staggerwings ever built, the last being delivered on 17 June 1949. More than 100 Staggerwings are known to be flying in various parts of the world, and each October many examples gather at the Staggerwing Museum and Twin Beech 18 Society Fly-In at Tullahoma, Tennessee.

◀ Throw-over control yokes were popular in many aircraft designs of the 1930s – Beech retained this innovation post-war in its popular 'V'-tail Bonanza *(GPJ)*

▲ Mike Bell, owner of this Staggerwing, is dwarfed beside the cowling that houses the aircraft's powerful 275 hp Jacobs radial engine *(GPJ)*

Arriving home – Mike Bell carefully flies his Staggerwing over the road, power lines and hangars on to Lodi's narrow runway, its home in California *(GPJ)*

▼

Waco UBF-2 (1932)

Clayton J. Brukner and Elwood J. Junkin's Waco Aircraft Company was set up in 1920. As 'Buck' Weaver had provided most of the necessary finance, the company was named after him (Waco is pronounced *Wah-Co*). Weaver also taught both Brukner and Junkin to fly. In 1923 the company was renamed the Advance Aircraft Company, and it moved within the state of Ohio from Medina to Troy. Weaver was no longer involved in the small operation, and Brukner and Junkin were the main figures.

However, the Waco tag had stuck, and in June 1929 the name was officially changed from Advance Aircraft back to Waco Aircraft Company. In 1933 it reported a profit of $67 733, a near 7% increase over the 1932 profit. The company was highly regarded, and one of the best-known American manufacturers of what are now called general aviation aircraft. It had survived the years of the Depression, and was building aircraft for both the commercial sector (including Northwest Airways) and private owners. All of its designs were biplanes, and the company was building more civil aircraft than any two of its competitors combined.

Although the Waco UBF-2 was one of the most popular sport biplanes produced by the company at Troy, only eighteen examples were built in the 1930s. Given the name 'Tourist', the UBF-2 was unquestionably the finest sport biplane of its time. It could seat three, with the pilot behind the two passengers side-by-side in the front cockpit, and had a 220 hp Continental R-670-6A providing a 132 mph top speed and 116 mph at the cruise. However, it wasn't the straight and level speed that distinguished this aircraft, but its handling and performance during aerial manoeuvres. The Clark 'Y' aerofoil helped considerably, enabling the aircraft to take off and land within 100 ft and giving it a 1500 ft/min rate of climb. Its aerobatic capabilities were some of the best at the time, thanks to a relatively short 29 ft 7 in wingspan and compact 20 ft 6 in length. Its empty weight was just 1600 lb, but at gross it was 2300 lb.

These were undoubtedly major reasons for the US Navy taking more than a passing interest in the tiny Waco UBF-2 in 1934. On 17 February two were delivered to the Naval Air Station at Anacostia (District of Columbia), and designated the XJW-1. They

A relatively short 29 ft 7 in wingspan characterises the Waco UBF-2 *(GPJ)*

The Waco UBF-2 was one of the few products of the famous Troy, Ohio-based aircraft manufacturer to be given a name, the *Tourist (GPJ)*

were fitted with hooks on their upper wings and used to indoctrinate new pilots into the 'hook-on' procedure aboard the US Navy's airship USS *Macon*, and for preparing airmen for solo in the Curtiss F9C-2 Sparrowhawk fighters. The XJW-1 was powered by a 210 hp Continental engine and replaced the Navy's Consolidated N2Y-1.

When new the UBF-2 seen here sold for $5025; its value today is difficult to determine but must be ten times that. Although initially designated a UBF-2 and completed at Troy on 8 April 1933, this particular aircraft (NC13071, serial number 3689), received slight factory modifications, its designation changing to a UBF-3 as it became the prototype for the similar Waco UMF-3, YMF-3 and YMF-5 series of aircraft. The YMF-5 is the Waco variant that was still being built in 2001 by the Classic Aircraft Corporation in Michigan, set up in 1983 by Richard Kettles and Michael Dow. The modern YMF-5 is powered by a 275-hp Jacobs R-755-B2 radial engine and more than 70 have been sold.

In 1938, NC13071 was seriously damaged in a fire following a

crash resulting from pilot error during low-level aerobatics. The remains were stored, until in 1976 they were acquired by Marion 'Curly' Havelaar, who started on a complete rebuild. By 1987, having rebuilt the steel tube fuselage and landing gear. Havelaar decided to sell the aircraft. The Woods family from California took it on, and put it in the hands of Glen Styles, the chief restoration engineer at Aero Meridian in Scottsdale, Arizona, who completed the project to the high standard seen here. Almost exactly 57 years to the day since it rolled off the Waco assembly line, UBF-2 NC13071 flew again on 10 April 1990.

Chris Woods, a director of television commercials, was the owner of the Waco at the time of the photo shoot in September 2000. He kept it at Gnoss County airport at Novato, just to the east of San Francisco, where it shared hangar space with his father's Spitfire Mk XVIe (NX721WK/SL), although this was sold soon after to a Canadian owner. It was in the Bay Area close to Novato that the accompanying pictures were shot.

Despite its aerobatic potential, Chris Wood prefers to treat his Waco UBF-2 gently, as befits a classic *(GPJ)*

BELOW RIGHT:
Instrumentation in the rear pilot's cockpit of Chris Wood's Waco UBF-2 is minimal *(GPJ)*

Chris Wood flies his highly manoeuvrable Waco UBF-2 over one of the many tributaries that flow into San Francisco Bay *(GPJ)*

Waco UIC (1933)

Open-cockpit flying was fine for air show performers and other exhibitionists. Waco's customers in 1933 were a discerning bunch and made the company move swiftly to cabin models. The Waco QDC and UEC of 1931 and 1932 were intended to set the standard.

With four seats in a comfortable enclosed cabin, 1933's Waco UIC had further refinements including a more streamlined fuselage, propeller spinner, full-skirt bump engine cowling, wing and landing gear fairings, wheel spats, wing-strut flaps and better interior. These improvements helped add another 10 mph to the UIC's cruise performance when compared with similar Waco predecessors. During 1933 Waco built and sold more than 70 UIC models.

The featured aircraft, Waco UIC NC13563 (serial number 3817), was delivered new in 1933 to G. Allan Hancock for his flight training school at Santa Maria, California, which he had founded in the 1920s. Hancock went to Waco's factory at Troy to collect the aircraft, and flew it back to California, keeping it in his fleet until 1935. He sold it to Bud Foster who then based it at Dicer Field, just to the south of what is now LAX (Los Angeles International Airport), where he used it for general aerial-charter work. It was then used for flight training until 1940, when it crashed on the beach near San Diego.

Rebuilt by Lou Leibee, it was sold to a doctor in Bakersfield, before being requisitioned for the civilian pilot training program. It was based at Lone Pine in California, but in 1943 was donated to a college at Cedar City in Utah, where it remained, unflown, until the mid-1960s. 'Boy' Good then bought it, restored it and sold it to Gordon Cragg, an aircraft dealer based in Houston, Texas. Jon Aldrich bought it from Cragg in 1987, and flew it home to Pine Mountain Lake in the foothills of the Sierra Nevada in California, where it has lived ever since.

Aldrich, 65, moved to Pine Mountain Lake, one of the first successful American fly-in communities, in 1980. He trained in a Piper PA-12 Super Cruiser in the early 1960s. Aldrich had lent his instructor the money to buy the aircraft, the deal being that he would teach Aldrich to fly.

Aldrich bought a Waco UPF-7 and a Ryan Navion early in his flying career and started buying and selling vintage aircraft parts, setting up his company, Vintage Aero Supply, at Orange County Airport, now John Wayne, in southern Los Angeles. He kept the UPF-7 until 1987, when he sold it to an enthusiast in Vermont. It was a fateful delivery flight; crossing the continental divide the UPF-7 crashed. The pilot escaped with minor injuries but the aircraft caught fire and was destroyed. Aldrich rescued a few small items from the wreckage, including the spinner, which is now fitted to his UIC.

He moved his business to Costa Mesa and then to his home at Pine Mountain Lake, switching sales to mail order. He has owned several other aircraft, including a Cessna 175 which he had converted to a tail-dragger by Bowlin Conversions in Ohio, and another Cessna, a 1959, straight-tail, 150 (N5813E), which still shares the hangar with his Waco. The Cessna is the 315th built.

His interest in Wacos started with his UPF-7, which he owned for 18 years, until his desire for the greater comfort of a cabin led him to contact the National Waco Club. He also wanted a Waco

with a Continental radial rather than a Jacobs. In late 1987, he flew to Houston and bought his UIC on the spot. It had originally been fitted with a seven-cylinder 210 hp Continental with 'greasers' on the overhead cam, but one of Aldrich's first tasks was to re-engine it with its current 220 hp Continental W-670-6.

Other jobs completed when he got the UIC back home included recovering the fabric on the wings and tail, which led to the discovery of a broken spar – and the discarded skin of a rattlesnake in the rear fuselage, presumably from its sojourn in Texas.

The original log books were missing, so Aldrich has had to piece together its history. He knows it is still in its original factory colours, with silver wings and vermilion fuselage. The airframe has about 1500 hours of which Aldrich has flown about 400, mainly on shorter flights in the California area. He has 5000-plus hours total flying time in his log book.

Pilot's window wound down, Jon Aldrich enjoys his Waco UIC in the warm evening sunshine over his Pine Mountain Lake home *(GPJ)*

Plenty of roof glazing gives the cockpit of the Waco UIC a very airy feel – note the throw-over yoke and the elliptical instrument panel, similar to the one fitted to Chris Wood's 1932 Waco UBF-2 *(GPJ)*

ABOVE TOP:
The vermilion of Jon Aldrich's Waco UIC is the same as when it was delivered to its first owner at Santa Maria, California, in 1933 *(GPJ)*

The tail 'feathers' of Waco UIC NC13563 were constructed like those of most other light aircraft of the 1930s, with a wood and steel tube structure covered with fabric *(GPJ)*

Waco YKS-6 (1934)

Built in Troy, Ohio, in 1936, N16512 was a worker, hauling cargo and passengers in Alaska for 30 years *(CRS)*

Lightning struck twice in 1934 for the Waco Aircraft Company. The UKC cabin biplane introduced early in the year was a success and so was the follow-up YKC. In fact, the YKC – powered by the new 225 hp Jacobs L-4 radial – became Waco's best-selling aircraft that year.

With a few minor modifications, it returned to production the following year as the YKC-S. It joined the UKC-S and CJC-S as one of Waco's Standard Cabin models for 1935.

While it lacked the finesse of the UOC and YOC, the top of Waco's Custom Cabin line for that year, the YKC-S offered plenty for the money. The discount price, possible through modifications primarily intended to cut production costs, made it especially attractive.

Offered again in 1936 with enough changes to warrant a new designation, the Jacobs L-4-powered YKC-S became the YKS-6, one of the most popular cabin Wacos ever. No wonder: the retail price at the factory was a very reasonable $4995.

Two of the most obvious changes from the YKC-S to the YKS-6 were the redesigned main gear and a smooth cowling minus the rocker-box bumps. The gear, which had an 87-in tread, now had two streamlined legs braced to the fuselage in a tripod form, enabling the YKS-6 to handle a heavier gross weight.

It came with the standard two-colour factory paint job; silver wings and choice of red, black, grey, green or blue fuselage. A Hartzell wooden propeller was standard, but a ground-adjustable Hamilton-Standard or fixed pitch Curtiss-Reed metal version were optional.

Creature comforts, such as good visibility and a well-insulated and ventilated cabin, were other selling points. Other modern touches included Westport, Lear or RCA radios; a Lux fire extinguisher; Grimes retractable landing lights; and night emergency parachute flares mounted inside the rear fuselage.

Later versions of the YKS-6 (serial number 4419 onwards) were configured to seat five; but that was possible only by cutting back on fuel and baggage. The normal fuel capacity was 70 gallons: 35 in the root end of each upper wing. A 100-gallon capacity was available by adding a 15-gallon tank to each lower wing root.

The rugged, reliable YKS-6 could be adapted for a variety of uses, including cargo-hauler, air ambulance and air taxi, on either wheels or floats. In fact, the float-equipped version was a big seller, delivered worldwide, especially to Canada, South America and Australia.

The YKC/YKS-series type certificate was issued by the Civil Aeronautics Authority in April 1934, with amendments added annually as new models were introduced. The models approved under the original type certificate were the YKC in 1934, the YKC-S in 1935, the YKS-6 in 1936 and the ZKS-6 also in 1936.

According to Waco records, 65 YKS-6 were built but only 15 remained active on the American register 65 years later.

One of these is N16512 (4504), a 1936 model owned by Jerry Hanson of Las Vegas when these photographs were taken. It is one of the rare flying ambulance versions of the YKS-6. Unlike other cabin Wacos, it has entry doors on both sides of the fuselage and a luggage compartment with a fold-down door behind the main cabin on the left.

It was purchased new from the factory in 1936 by Western Flying Service of Denver, Colorado. Incredibly, it spent more than thirty years earning its keep in Alaska and was only brought down to the 'lower 48' and restored in 1989.

The YKS-6 sold for only $4995 new in 1936, but Hanson reportedly sold N16512 for around $85 000 in 1997.

▶ The business end of the Waco YKS-6 with its 245 hp Jacobs L-4/R-755-7 radial at full bore *(CRS)*

This colourful Waco YKS-6 was owned by Jerry Hanson of Las Vegas, Nevada, when photographed, but was later sold in Europe *(CRS)*

▼

Kinner Sportwing B2R (1934)

The Sportwing was originally manufactured by the Kinner Airplane & Motor Company based in Glendale, California *(CRS)*

A sport version of the Kinner Sportster, the Sportwing B2 made its debut in 1934. Its hallmarks were streamlined landing gear spats, an Naca-type bumped cowl, and a five-cylinder, 125 hp, Kinner B5 radial engine.

The strut-braced low-wing monoplane offered side-by-side seating for two in an open cockpit. Although only eight examples were built, the Sportwing B2 was popular with West Coast pilots and led the Kinner Airplane & Motor Corporation of Glendale, Califonia, to eventually develop the Sportwing B2R.

But as of January 1937, Kinner hadn't built an aircraft in more than a year and was in danger of going out of business. A modified version of the B2, the prototype B2R was fitted with a 160 hp Kinner R5 engine.

Like its predecessors, it had an enthusiastic but limited following among Californian sportsmen. Several were built, but when the anticipated demand failed to materialise, Kinner went bankrupt and closed its doors.

The rights to the Sportster and Sportwing were acquired by Kinner's long-time competitor, the Timm Aircraft Co., also of Glendale, California. When the design was revived, it was designated the Timm Model 160.

Timm tried to interest the Army in it as a primary trainer but the side-by-side seating was deemed unsatisfactory. Though it was converted to a tandem, the Army chose the Fairchild series of primary trainers.

Records indicated that only four Timm 160/Kinner B2R models were built. It had a roomy cockpit with tiny, triangle-shaped access doors on either side and a 41-gallon fuel tank located between the instrument panel and firewall.

Despite having an open cockpit, it was not a helmet and goggles aircraft, thanks to the shape of its wrap-around windshield. In addition to a glove compartment-size baggage area behind the headrest, the Sportwing B2R had two 50 lb baggage compartments hidden beneath lift-up lids in each wing stub.

This 1934 Kinner Sportwing B2R is owned by Dale Miller of Claremont, California, a 72-year-old retired fireman and paramedic. Beginning in 1988, he spent 12 years building it up from the rusted hulk of a 1934 Kinner Sportster K.

Miller says it would be most accurate to describe it as a scratch-build hybrid, a Sportwing built from a Sportster. Besides the engine, the only original parts are the engine mount, fuel tank and windshield; everything else was handmade from original Kinner plans.

This was the second Sportwing that Miller 'rebuilt'. The first, 15 years earlier, was a Sportwing B2 for someone in Oklahoma. Both the B2 and B2R are the only known examples of their kind flying today.

Miller began the restoration by obtaining copies of the original Kinner drawings for the Sportwing, which had been in storage with the FAA in San Diego since Kinner folded. He then welded up an airframe that was completely new except for three lengths of original tubing.

He made several modifications to the plans, including the addition of a heavier, five-cylinder, 160 hp Kinner R55 radial and installing two nine-gallon auxiliary fuel tanks in the wing root baggage compartments. The Kinner also features a steerable tailwheel and Cessna 310 wheels and brakes.

The tail section fairings and two-piece bumped cowl were handmade by an 80-year-old craftsman from Gardena, California. Also custom-made was the 94-in wood propeller and Sportwing's signature wheelpants and spats.

Folding wings were standard on the Sportster, but not the Sportwing. Miller added them to make room in his hangar for his other aircraft.

Folding the wings takes about two minutes per wing. Using a special crank, you remove a machined pin that locks the two halves of the mainspar together above each main gear, then lift and fold the wing back along the fuselage.

The aileron cables go slack and a bracing bar is used to hold the wingtip off the tail and keep the trailing edge of the wing stub from puncturing the top of the wing.

A point of interest on the Sportwing is the familiar shape of the tail – it is almost exactly the same as that of a Ryan STA, which was designed by former Kinner engineers in 1936.

Since the first flight in 2000, Miller has logged about 50 hours in the aircraft. It gets off the ground in about 150 ft, cruises at 115 mph, and burns about 10 gallons an hour.

Owner Dale Miller says the thick, heavy wing makes the Kinner rock-solid even in turbulent air *(CRS)*

Dale Miller spent 12 years rebuilding this 1934 Kinner Sportwing B2R almost from scratch *(CRS)*

The engine beneath the roomy, hand-made bumped cowling is a five-cylinder, 160 hp Kinner R55 radial *(CRS)*

Boeing 75 Stearman (1935)

The Boeing 75 made its debut in 1935, a year after Stearman Aircraft of Wichita, Kansas, became a subsidiary of the Boeing Airplane Company of Seattle. Both had been part of United Aircraft & Transport, and joined forces when the conglomerate broke up in 1934.

The prototype of the 75 was the 1933 70, which had evolved from the Stearman C series. The 75 itself was first certificated as a commercial aircraft in 1939, but it was in military service that it made its invaluable contribution to aviation.

The US Army and Navy both employed it as their main primary trainer before and throughout the second world war. As a result, the otherwise outdated biplane was mass-produced at several plants, 10 346 of them being built from 1939 to 1945.

The 75 has suffered an identity crisis all its life. It is commonly referred to as a Stearman, but is actually a Boeing – the Stearman Company having been renamed the Wichita division of Boeing in 1939. It was later given the name Kaydet to reflect its role in military service.

In fact, the 75 was given eight different factory model numbers and nine basic military designations despite only minor differences (usually engines). The E75, for example, was called a PT-13D by the army, and an N2S-5 by the navy. Most people today refer to them all with the generic term: Stearman PT-17.

The military paid between $7713 and $10 412 during the war for the various versions of the 75. But when thousands of them were made surplus, they were picked up for pennies on the dollar by scrapdealers, barnstormers and cropdusters.

Stearmans dominated the cropdusting business for nearly 20 years after the war. It is primarily these aircraft that survive today, with more than 2000 of them in America alone.

Most Stearmans flying today have been restored to original military standards as either Army PT-17 or Navy N2S-3 warbirds. What is unusual about the Stearman featured here is that it is a working aircraft rather than a showplane.

Painted in a John Deere tractor colour scheme of green and yellow, it is one of dozens of aircraft that tow banners over San Diego's stadiums and beaches. Nicknamed *Miss Kandi*, the highly modified 1945 Boeing 75 Stearman belongs to Aerial Advertising, a banner-towing operation based at nearby Gillespie Field. Both the aircraft and the business are owned by 38-year-old Kent Parish, of San Diego.

A cropduster in an earlier life, *Miss Kandi* is powered by a 450 hp Pratt & Whitney R-985 radial assisted by special high-lift wings for short take-off and landing. The fuselage has been metallised, the front seat faired over, and a banner-towing rig attached to the tail, earning it a restricted category licence.

Pilot Mark Madden shows off the Stearman over El Capitan Reservoir near Aerial Advertising's home base, Gillespie Field in El Cajon, California *(CRS)*

Among *Miss Kandi*'s many modifications for banner-towing are squared-off, highlift STOL wings, and ailerons on both the upper and lower wings *(CRS)*

The letters used to spell out the messages on banners are made of rip-stop nylon and are 7 ft tall by 3 ft wide; nylon strips at the top and bottom are used to clip them to a fiberglass rod that runs the length of the banner. A typical message averages between 30 and 60 letters and is about 150 ft long and weighs between 60 and 80 lb.

To hold the banner upright behind the aircraft and to keep it from twisting once air-borne, a metal pole weighted at the bottom is attached to the front of the banner. To keep it flying straight and taut, two sections of fabric called a tail chute are attached to the end to create drag.

While one person lays the banner out for pick-up (the line connected to the banner is strung across two 7-ft-tall poles set about 20 ft apart), the pilot checks the tow rig on the Stearman.

One end of the line is attached to a fitting on the tailwheel with about 30 ft of coiled line loosely clipped beneath the horizontal stabiliser. The business end of the line, which has a three-pronged aluminium grappling hook on it, is carried inside the cockpit.

When all is ready, the pilot takes off and circles around for the pick-up. With the Stearman throttled back to 70 mph, he crosses the runway threshold, descends to about 25 ft off the deck and lines up to split the two poles.

Just before reaching them, he tosses the hook over the side, adds full power and yanks back on the stick, pulling the Stearman up into a 45° climb. The hook should fall cleanly, the seal that holds the coiled line under the stabiliser breaking and allowing the tow line to pay out to its full length.

The steep climb causes the hook to swing forward and snag the line stretched between the poles. As the Stearman climbs away, the slack in the line is taken up and the banner unfurls as it is snatched into the air.

Once the banner is aloft, the flying shifts into slow motion, with cruising between 40 and 55 mph for hours at a time.

To release the banner the pilot approaches the drop point at 55 mph and at about 200 to 300 ft above ground level, descending to 20 ft as he approaches the pick-up poles. He then pulls the release handle on the floor to disconnect the tow line, adds power and circles to land.

Aerial Advertising's sign on the fuselage tells it all *(CRS)*

Miss Kandi is powered by a 450 hp Pratt & Whitney R-985 radial, which gives the biplane power to spare *(CRS)*

The Stearman's upper wing had a span of 32.2 ft, the bottom 31.2 ft, for a total wing area of 297.6 sq. ft *(CRS)*

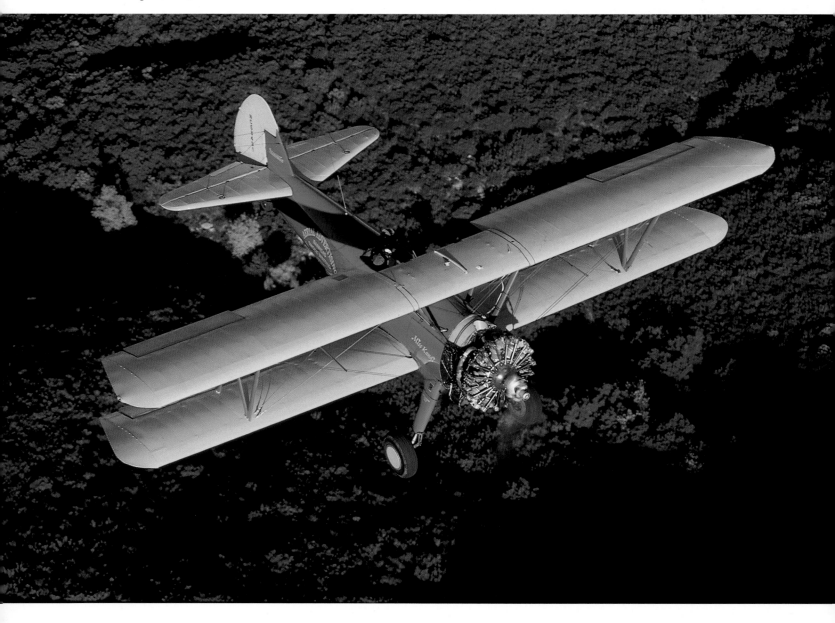

The banner tow line is attached to the aircraft from behind the tailwheel and is carried loosely coiled beneath the horizontal stabiliser until dropped *(CRS)*

Instead of fabric stretched taut over stringer and longerons, *Miss Kandi*'s 24.8ft fuselage has been metallised *(CRS)*

Stearmans were mass-produced at several plants during the second world war, with 10 346 of them being built, ranging in price from $7713 to $10 412 *(CRS)*

Douglas DC-3 (1935)

'Probably the deepest and most thorough DC-3 restoration that has ever been undertaken.' These are the words of James Ray, the manager of Delta Air Lines' museum restoration projects. It was a proud day for him and his team in October 1999 just after the 70th anniversary of Delta Air Services' first scheduled passenger flight on 17 June 1929. After tens of thousands of man hours of work, Delta's DC-3, its 'Ship 41', flew again for the first time at the airline's headquarters and the world's largest single airline hub operation, Atlanta Hartsfield International Airport, Georgia.

This particular DC-3 was one of the original five delivered to Delta in 1940, registered NC28341 (serial number 3278). Delivery date was 23 December, and it flew its first commercial service on Christmas Day. For eighteen years it served the airline before being sold to North Central Airlines.

During the late 1980s a group of Delta retirees had been researching some of its former aircraft and in 1990 discovered the former Ship 41, by then N29PR in the colours of Air Puerto Rico and derelict at San Juan. It took two years of negotiations to acquire it, but in 1993 their efforts were rewarded and in mid-1993 Ship 41 arrived back at Atlanta at the start of what was to be a six-year restoration. The work was slow, thorough and meticulous, starting with minimal support from Delta, most of the work was carried out by retired and current employees in their own time. However, as the enormity of the task and the likely cost and time became apparent, Delta became more supportive of the project, realising the huge publicity potential of having one of its original aircraft, in an airworthy condition, to promote the airline all over America.

Delta had already shown its colours as far as its heritage was concerned. The hangar in which Ship 41 was being restored was one of its original 1940s hangars at Atlanta that had been preserved. There, in the Delta Air Museum, the original Huff-Daland Duster biplane was already housed; in non-airworthy condition. It had been used by Delta's predecessor in 1924 to start the world's first aerial crop-dusting operation.

The other aircraft in the museum, kept airworthy and wearing

After six years of the most thorough workmanship imaginable the restored Delta Air Lines DC-3 flew again for the first time at Atlanta, Georgia, in October 1999 *(DAL)*

the 1929 colours of Delta Air Services, is a 1931 Curtiss-Wright Travel Air 6B Sedan, representative of the Travel Air Model S-6000B with which Delta's first passenger services began in 1929. This aircraft was bought by Delta from one of their former airline captains, Doug Rounds, in 1985. Its guise as S-6000B BC8878 isn't its true identity.

James Ray and his team were also responsible for the restoration of a Lockheed L-1011 TriStar cockpit that was then donated to one of Disney's American theme parks. A non-airworthy Heath Parasol is also kept in the Atlanta museum, built and flown by a former Delta employee.

The highlight for Ray and his team came in July 2000, when DC-3 Ship 41 and the Travel Air were flown north from Atlanta to attend the Air Venture Fly-In at Oshkosh. The DC-3 scooped a Special Judges' Antique Choice award in recognition of the superb restoration work.

A project of the size of that undertaken on the DC-3 involved a huge team effort. The airline, many of its employees – both on a paid and voluntary basis – and many retired personnel were involved. Corrosion in the cockpit area led to a total rebuild and the wings and most of the fuselage were re-skinned. The cockpit is not 1940s original, as small radios from the latter part of the twentieth century and nav/com equipment have been discreetly installed. The old analogue instruments however, still dominate the instrument panel (it can be flown only under visual flight rules).

Seats have been rebuilt, with modern sound-proofing and fire-proofing insulation fitted inside the cockpit and passenger areas. An exact reproduction of the 1940s galley was possible thanks to detailed period photos. Seats and cabin upholstery were made from new to 1940s patterns, and Delta even had forties-era uniforms made. Zero-houred engines and accessories were supplied by JRS Enterprises of Minnesota, landing gear and hydraulic valves by Basler at Oshkosh, and radios and other equipment was donated by Collins.

Landmarks in the restoration were the signing-off of the landing gear by the FAA after trial retractions; the switching on of the DC-3's electrical power systems; and finally, in March 1999, Ship 41 being rolled out of the restoration hangar on its own wheels and its engines fired up for the first time.

The test pilot was picked from Delta's huge air-crew establishment at Atlanta. Bill Mercure, now a Boeing 767 training captain, has loads of tail-dragger experience, much of it on his Pitts Special, and more than 2000 hours on other DC-3 aircraft over the past thirty years. Delta chartered another DC-3 from Ron Alexander, also a Delta pilot, at Griffin to the south of Atlanta for familiarisation training for Mercure and the rest of his team before the first post-restoration flight.

The achievement of Ray and his colleagues is remarkable. He is at pains to point out that it was a huge group effort, with considerable team spirit involved. 'We did the restoration not only for the people at Delta who came before us, but for those who will be here long after we have gone,' he said. These words could just as easily apply to all the aircraft featured in this book.

Many documents and photographs were studied to ensure authenticity during the restoration. Delta Air Lines' 1940s corporate logo, now adorning Ship 41's rear fuselage, was copied from period photographs such as this *(DAL)*

Not completely 1940s original, but NC28341's cockpit has to comply with twenty-first century air traffic requirements. Despite several digital instruments, there are still plenty of old-fashioned analogue dials and control wheels, along with those stalky, charismatic throttle, mixture and pitch control levers in the central console *(DAL)*

The ravages of time and corrosion since 1940 had wreaked severe damage on NC28341 – much of the DC-3's airframe, including the fuselage skin and most of the cockpit, had to be replaced by Delta during the restoration *(GPJ)*

Much time has been lavished by Delta on making the interior of its DC-3 as authentic as possible – this view looking rearward shows the seats, interior trim, hat-racks and galley *(DAL)*

OPPOSITE PAGE:
The quality and depth of the restoration by Delta's team under the leadership of James

Ray is reflected in the DC-3's sparkling finish *(GPJ)*

Delta's Bill Mercure eases NC28341 Ship 41 into the skies over Atlanta during its first post-restoration flight *(DAL)*

Spartan 7W Executive (1936)

If ever an aircraft oozed style it is the Spartan 7W Executive, the almost art-deco derivative of Jim (J. B.) Ford's 1934–35 design. The prototype first flew in January 1936 at Tulsa, Oklahoma. It was also a highly advanced design, being the first all-metal four-seat monoplane on the American market, and prompted the development of several military export models.

The prototype, designated the 7-X, was powered by a 285 hp Jacobs L-5 engine. More power was needed, and when the 400 hp, nine-cylinder, Pratt & Whitney Wasp Junior engine was fitted, the designation became the Spartan 7W, 'W' identifying the Wasp installation. The prototype of this definitive version first flew in September 1936.

Retired newspaper executive Kent Blankenburg, the owner of our featured example, believes that from a total production of 34, there are about twelve left, only six of which are thought to be airworthy. NC17667 now has about 5000 hours total, of which 500 have been logged by Blankenburg and his wife Sandy since they became custodians – they prefer this to the word *owner* – in early 1994. The list of customers for this unique, 200 mph-plus leviathan of the mid-1930s was almost like a *Who's Who* of the American oil industry. It was unashamedly targeted at customers with plenty of money and impeccable taste. In 1937, Arlene Davis, sponsored by the Claude Drilling Co. of Tulsa, flew Executive NC17605 in the National Air Races. The King of Iraq also bought an Executive (serial number 7W-19) and named it *Eagle of Iraq*.

The Blankenburgs' Executive (7W-17) was built in 1939, towards the end of the type's production run – the approval certificate for the type expired in October 1941. It was one of three Executives exported to Canada and which served with the Royal Canadian Air Force as a liaison aircraft. Post-war it was owned by the Texaco Oil Company, and placed in the hands of Spartan Aircraft which had a major refurbishment programme in progress for Executives. This included flush riveting of the wing and tail leading edges. It was then owned for four or five years by Malcolm Jacobs, a Beech Staggerwing dealer in Missouri. When he died it was bought by the Lone Star Flight Museum, and in five years it flew only two ferry flights, from St Louis to Houston and then from Houston to Galveston. Kent and Sandy Blankenburg bought it in early 1994; they had been searching for a 7W Executive for several years, and had already seen five. At this time the aircraft had brown tinted windows and orange trim over the customary polished metal finish.

The Blankenburgs flew it to St Louis Obispo on the Californian coast for a major overhaul and refurbishment, and then to their home at Pine Mountain Lake in 1995. Subsequently it was taken to Alan Buchner's workshop in Fresno on several occasions for lots of small, detailed work, one of the few concessions to authenticity being the GPS antenna on top of the fuselage. It originally had a three-bladed propeller in the 1970s, but now has an 8 ft 6 in Hamilton 2D-30 two-blade.

Kent Blankenburg believes this Executive is mechanically very sound – he and Sandy regularly fly it to air shows, fly-ins and other events throughout the U.S.A. The air-to-air photos show the elliptical, almost Spitfire-like, wing form. This helps give the aircraft its superb performance with a high-speed cruise of 208 mph (2200 rpm at 9600 ft); economy cruise at 65% power at 190 mph, and range (at 65% power) of 1000 miles. Climb rate to a 9600 ft cruise altitude is nine minutes, maintaining a 128 mph climb speed. Landing speed is 65 mph, and the Spartan 7W Executive can take off and land at its 4400 lb gross weight in 600 ft.

Fitting in superbly with Sandy Blankenburg's art deco collection of airline and other memorabilia in one of the family's two pristine hangars at Pine Mountain Lake, the polished-metal Executive is 'sister ship' to several other classic polished-metal aircraft in their custody – a Lockheed 12 Cessna 195, two extremely rare Luscombe Phantoms, a Luscombe 8, and, perhaps a little out of place, a Republic Seabee. They employ someone full time to care for and polish them.

The main hazard at their idyllic setting amid the flying community at Pine Mountain Lake is the deer from the forest who saunter across the runway in the morning and evening – and then come to feast on the lawns in front of the hangars!

The almost Spitfire-like, elliptical wing form of the Spartan Executive can really be appreciated only in the air *(GPJ)*

Its all-metal construction, four seats and low-wing monoplane design made the Spartan Executive highly advanced for 1936 *(GPJ)*

RIGHT:
The interior of this Spartan Executive is as pristine as its shining, polished metal exterior. There is only a single port-side access door, and as in many similar contemporary types, there is a throw-over control yoke *(GPJ)*

FAR RIGHT:
A 400 hp Pratt & Whitney Wasp powers the Spartan Executive, here springing to life in a cloud of fuel and oil *(GPJ)*

OPPOSITE PAGE:
Over the foothills of California's Sierra Nevada mountains, Kent and Sandy Blankenburg's Spartan Executive is one of only about six airworthy examples *(GPJ)*

Grumman G-21 Goose (1937)

Although designed and produced for the civil market, the Grumman Goose amphibian also found unexpected favour with the military when it appeared just before the second world war. A contemporary of the Douglas DC-3, the prototype (N16910, serial number 1001) first flew on 29 May 1937. Named *Grey Goose* by company founder LeRoy Grumman, it was delivered to co-owners Wilton Lloyd Smith, a financier, and Marshall Field III on 16 July.

The Goose was Grumman's first monoplane, and its first twin-engine design, following several famous Grumman biplane fighter-bombers such as the F.3F Gulfhawk. Work on the Goose design started in 1936 at the instigation of Grover Loening, the U.S.A.'s best-known seaplane designer in the early 1930s, who had wealthy customers looking for a 'modern' aircraft to replace the Loening Air Yacht and Loening Commuter amphibians they operated.

The customer list numbered ten in September 1937. It included Lord Beaverbrook, the British publishing magnate (his aircraft was G-AFCH in October 1937, followed by G-AFKJ in 1938 after the first one had been sold); Wilton Lloyd-Smith; Gar Wood, a famous speedboat racer of the time; Powell Crosley Jr (president of the Crosley Radio Corporation, now the giant Avco); and Boris Sergievsky, the test pilot for Sikorsky.

Two Pratt & Whitney Wasp Junior SB (R-985) engines, each rated between 400 and 450 hp, powered the Goose. It was of all-metal construction, except for the fabric-covered control surfaces, and seated two crew and six passengers. Between 1937 and October 1945 a total of 345 Goose were built. Many served with the military – particularly in naval operations – in Peru, Portugal, Bolivia, Canada, Argentina, Brazil, Cuba, Paraguay, France, Japan and Sweden. The US Navy was also a major customer, where the type was designated the JRF-1 and -5. The US Coast Guard called it the JRF-2, the Army Air Corps the OA-9.

Many bush- and island-based airlines have used the Grumman Goose as a passenger/freight work-horse. Two of the best known were Avalon Air Transport, later Catalina Airlines, in California, and Antilles Air Boats, later the Virgin Islands Seaplane Shuttle, in the West Indies. The Goose has been used in the Canadian and Alaskan outback for nearly fifty years.

There are thought to be about 40 Goose surviving in America, and a further 20 in Canada. The featured example is owned and flown by Bill Rose, an Illinois-based industrialist, who spends much of the winter at his Florida home at Marco Island and uses his Goose to commute. He also owns several other warbirds and classics.

N600ZE is a G-21A Goose (serial number B-100), built in 1944 as one of 190 JRF-5 models for the US Navy. It isn't a stock Goose; few today are. In 1969 McKinnon Enterprises, of Sandy, Oregon, made several modifications to N600ZE. Other companies including Volpar, of Van Nuys, California; McKinnon-Viking Enterprises of Sidney, British Columbia; and Marshall of Cambridge, England, have done engine conversions. McKinnon in the U.S.A. started with an engine retrofit programme for the Goose in 1958, in one case replacing the two radial engines with four 340 hp Lycoming GSO-480 units. Engines were changed on many other Goose by McKinnon over the years, mainly two Pratt & Whitney PT6A-20 turbo-props instead of the radial Wasp. The company also fitted retractable wing-tip floats and advanced flap devices, modifications now fitted to N600ZE, helping to enhance its performance. Original Pratt & Whitney radial engines are retained on this example throughout.

▲
Bill Rose's Goose N600ZE was built in 1944 as one of 190 military JRF-5 aircraft for the US Navy. Goose production totalled 345 *(GPJ)*

Opposite Page:
At home on the water, Bill Rose's Grumman G-21 Goose accelerates up onto the step just before lifting off from Lake Parker in Florida *(GPJ)*

▶
Demonstrating the reinforced hull of the Goose and those big, arched, almost cathedral-like front cockpit windows *(GPJ)*

Luscombe 8A (1937)

Don Luscombe's first production aircraft was the high-wing monoplane Phantom in 1934. Described as a thoroughbred, it was also expensive and tricky to fly. Don had learnt his trade as an associate of Monocoupe at Moline, Illinois. He is widely credited with the idea of enclosing the cabin under a high-wing monoplane design, at a time when contemporaries were still churning out biplanes. He also understood the need for economy in construction to keep the unit price down. In 1933 he left Monocoupe and moved to Kansas where he set up shop to experiment with his all-metal Phantom design. Twenty-two Phantoms were built, followed by the Model 4, before he turned his attention in 1937 to the more basic Model 8.

NX1304, the prototype Luscombe 8, first flew in December of that year, fitted with a 50 hp Continental A-50 engine. The prototype 8A soon followed, with a more powerful Continental A-65 engine, but still a side-by-side two-seat, cabin taildragger with metal airframe, but fabric-covered strut-braced high wings. It was unique at the time, and between 1938 and 1942, 1112 were built by the Luscombe Airplane Development Corporation, first just the 8A, but then derivatives such as the 8B, 8C and the 8D, which was named the Silvaire.

Production ceased in 1942 following the entry of America into the second world war, but in 1945 production resumed at Dallas, Texas, such was the demand for the little Luscombe 8. Its main competitor at the time was the Cessna 120, followed by the 140.

The highs of pre-war and immediate post-war production were soon to diminish as the market was swamped with two-seat recreational aircraft. In June 1949, Temco Engineering took over Luscombe Airplane and built the Luscombe Silvaire in parallel with the Globe Swift. Production rights passed to the Silvaire Aircraft Corporation in 1955, and it built a relatively small number of aircraft at Fort Collins, Colorado, until 1960. Total Luscombe 8 production by all manufacturers is thought to have totalled around 6000 aircraft, of which about 3000 still exist, 2400 of them registered in America.

Scott O'Brien's featured Luscombe 8A was built in 1945, the seventeenth aircraft off Luscombe's immediate post-war production line at Dallas. Fifty-five were built that year at the plant, and it was known by some as the Luscombe Master. The aircraft was appropriately named *Bad Habit* by the then owner Ken Demoteo, from whom O'Brien bought the Luscombe while it was still being rebuilt at Demoteo's Oceano workshop in

California in 1993. Demoteo is a master craftsman and had already lavished thousands of hours of work on the Luscombe rebuild, at the same time building a Vans RV-6 kitplane.

Cash-flow problems when he needed an engine for the Vans forced him to sell *Bad Habit*. O'Brien was looking for a cheap yet charismatic and practical light aircraft in which to build up his hours towards obtaining a commerical pilot's licence. When he got his first job as a first officer flying a corporate HS125 executive jet out of Palm Springs, half of the 650 hours of flying time he had accumulated had been in *Bad Habit*. In March 1995 he got a job with United Airlines – his father flies a Boeing 747-400 for United – flying in the right-hand seat of a Boeing 737-200. By the age of 33 he had become a captain on a 737 with Shuttle by United, their low-fare West Coast operation.

Despite the aura that goes with the captaincy, O'Brien loves the relaxation of flying *Bad Habit*, so basic and with its lack of equipment. Despite its small 65 hp engine, the Luscombe 8A is such a clean design that it can cruise at 100 mph, the engine turning at between 2100 and 2200 rpm. The maximum speed is 105 mph and the red line at 115 mph. Fuel and oil consumption is miserly at about four US gallons in the cruise, the engine taking only four quarts of oil. Like any tail-dragger, Scott says you have to make liberal use of the rudder in a Luscombe 8 – but give it too much rudder and you're into a ground loop! *Bad Habit* has cable-operated brakes, although O'Brien rarely uses them – there are no hydraulics, no electrics, and it has to be hand-swung to start. O'Brien believes that in a world where aviation maintenance bills can be horrendous, the less there is to go wrong the better.

The Luscombe 8A's stall is also quite dramatic compared with some more innocuous modern aircraft, with a pronounced wing-drop, and even with a quick response requiring a good 400 ft to recover. However, once in the cruise and away from the turbulent air of lower altitudes, the Luscombe 8 is a pleasure to fly because it isn't tail-down like a Cessna 140. O'Brien is also convinced that there's a step in the Luscombe's cruise performance, a speed of about 90 mph at which there's a sudden jump up to 100 mph.

In 1999 he reluctantly put *Bad Habit* up for sale, at an asking price of $28 000. He had taught his girlfriend to fly in *Bad Habit*, had married her and they now have two children. The Luscombe 8A was too small, so he has bought a Cessna 195, a loadhauler that could even carry a third child if the family grows. It has already been dubbed *Patience*.

OPPOSITE:
Much of the restoration work on this aircraft, part of the initial production batch of Luscombe 8A immediately post-war, was completed in the 1990s by Ken Demoteo *(GPJ)*

With a fairly narrow undercarriage track and a high wing, the Luscombe 8 can be tricky to land, even in a slight crosswind *(GPJ)*

Beautifully upholstered and finished but devoid of all but basic instrumentation, Scott O'Brien's Luscombe 8A *Bad Habit* was just what he wanted after flying commercially in a Boeing 737 as his day job *(GPJ)*

OPPOSITE PAGE:
Cockpit visibility is not good on the Luscombe 8A. However, it was an extremely popular design; Renaissance Aircraft plan to put the type back into production, with metal airframe components being made in the Czech Republic and assembly taking place in the U.S.A. *(GPJ)*

Despite having only a 65 hp Continental A65 engine, *Bad Habit* can cruise at 100 mph *(GPJ)*

Piper J-3 Cub (1937)

Featured on the front cover of our first book, *American Classics of the Air* (published by Airlife in January 2000), is a rare 1929 Fairchild 71 restored and flown by Tom Dixon. Regrettably this aircraft crashed near Rapid City, South Dakota, in July 1998 while he was flying to Oshkosh. He salvaged the remains and is into a lengthy rebuild. In the meantime he needed an aircraft to fulfil his flying desires and simply to keep current. His son, who was a student at California Polytechnic, wanted to obtain a pilot's licence, so one day in early January 2000 Dixon went to Brackett Field in California where a J-3 Cub had just been restored and was up for sale. Later that day he became the owner of a traditionally painted, impeccably restored, almost 'stock' 1946 Piper J-3C-65 Cub, NC98300. Its only concessions to modern requirements are a small electrical system and ribbed tyres, because, as Dixon says, 'you can't buy bald tyres as fitted to orginal J-3s any more'.

It was almost deja vu. As a child he had quickly developed an interest in aircraft modelling, fuelled by a visit with his father to Stockton airfield when he was only five or six to see Piper Cubs flying. In 1966 he got his student pilot's licence and with his friend Tom Murphy bought a Piper Cub for a mere $300, and taught themselves to fly in it, although Dixon didn't formally obtain his PPL until he could afford it in 1979! This Cub, his first (N2944), was sold on by Dixon and Murphy after about 18 months, for $1000. It is still flying in Oregon. In March 1967 Dixon acquired the remains of a Fairchild 24G which he started to restore, but in 1969 it had to be put on the back burner when he got married.

Dixon's latest Cub is one of the 19 888 J-3 Cubs of all models that are estimated to have been built for civil and military customers between 1937 and 1947. The Piper J-3 started out as the Taylor Aircraft Company J-3, designed by (or perhaps evolved by) William T. Piper, a company founded by brothers C. G. and Gordon Taylor in Rochester, New York, in the mid-1920s. After the stockmarket crash, Piper purchased the assets of the Taylors' company, including their E-2 Cub design in 1931 for $600. C. G. Taylor became president and treasurer of the new company. In 1935 Piper purchased Taylor's share in the company. C. G. Taylor went off to establish his Taylorcraft Aviation Company at Alliance, Ohio, the following year. Meanwhile, still as the Taylor Aircraft Company in early 1937 at Bradford, Pennsylvania, new, more reliable 40 and 50 hp engines were becoming available from Continental, Lycoming and the Franklin Aircooled Engine Company.

A potentially disastrous fire at the Bradford plant led to re-organisation. The company's name was changed to Piper Aircraft Corporation, and the operation moved to a former silk mill at Lock Haven, Pennsylvania. The first J-3 Cub was built in 1937 with one of the new engines and 687 were manufactured that year. In 1938 a J-3 Cub cost $1300 and production reached 736 aircraft. In 1940 the Cub was first approved by the Civil Aeronautics Authority (now the FAA) for use in the U.S.A., with a 65 hp engine.

Dixon keeps his Cub at Lodi, California, claiming that it helps him cope with his 'flying disease'. With its 65 hp engine, it's still a 'marginal' aircraft with two on board in hot weather. However, there's no disputing that it's great fun to fly, and takes the pressure off him having to complete his Fairchild 71 rebuild quickly! He flew it for about 50 hours in 2000, adding to the 1200 he has accumulated in his log book since the 1960s.

Tandem seating, dual control sticks, and dual throttles. But with no instruments directly in front of the rear occupant, they have to look over the shoulder of the person in front to find out the basics of flight conditions such as air speed and height *(GPJ)*

OPPOSITE PAGE:
Tom Dixon's virtually 'stock' Piper J-3C-65 Cub out on a beautifully kept grass area at Lodi, California. It is finished in traditional Cub yellow *(GPJ)*

Flown from the rear seat by Tom Dixon, the J-3C-65 Cub peacefully saunters low over the Californian countryside in the evening sunshine *(GPJ)*

Although now synonymous with the Cub, this eye-catching logo is believed not to have been adopted by Cub owners until fairly recently *(GPJ)*

Tom Dixon's first aircraft, in 1966, was a Cub which cost him and a friend $300. A J-3C-65 Cub in good condition like this can now cost around $30 000 *(GPJ)*

Tom Dixon's J-3C-65 Cub parked at its Lodi, California, base with some contemporary road transport *(GPJ)*

Aeronca KCA (1938)

In 1935 Aeronca (short for Aeronautical Corporation of America) was purchased by Walter Friedlander, who wanted to make it a dominant force in the aircraft industry.

Spurred on by the popularity of the competing Taylor J-2 Cub, Friedlander told his chief engineer, Roger Schlemmer, to come up with something new. The result was two very different aircraft – the Model L, a low-wing cabin type (featured in the first volume of *American Classics of the Air*), and the Model K, a high-wing cabin version based on earlier Aeroncas.

Work on the two aircraft began in October 1935, but despite the simplicity of its design, development of the K was dogged by engineering problems. It wasn't until January 1937, nearly a year after its first flight, that it finally entered production.

When it appeared with a price of $1480, it was greeted enthusiastically. It had a wider cabin for side-by-side seating, strut-braced wings and longer landing gear; it was also the first Aeronca with adjustable elevator trim tab.

There were other problems before production began at the Aeronca plant at Lunken airport in Cincinnati, Ohio, where a flood shut down the factory for two months. The first production Model K was finally completed on 15 April 1937.

Over the next nine months, 296 K type and nine of the float-equipped KS rolled off the line. While 1937 was a big year for the K, 1938 was a disappointment, with only 65 aircraft being built, the last eight of them being completed in early 1939.

In May 1938, the Model KC was introduced, powered by a 40 hp, single-ignition Continental A40-4. Essentially a refined version of the K, the KC had minor changes to the engine mount, cowling and gear.

Although the performance of both was virtually identical, the cost of replacing Aeronca's two-cylinder, 37/40 hp E-113C engine with the new Continental was added to the price of the KC. As a result, Aeronca sold only 19 KC aircraft in 1937, 13 in 1938 and three in 1939.

When a number of new 50 hp flat-four engines hit the market in late 1938, Aeronca responded with three new models: the KCA, powered by a Continental A50; the KF, powered by the Franklin AC-150; and the KM, powered by the Menasco M50. In April 1939, when Aeronca shut down the K-series production line, 62 of its KCA, nine KM and six KF had been built.

The 1938 Aeronca KCA shown here is owned by Terry Lucas and Tom Thompson of Oakdale, California.

It was the tenth of 62 KCAs built in 1938 and 1939, only 14 of which are still on the FAA register. When it was restored in 1998, it was painted in original factory colours: navy blue and Loening yellow.

Lucas and Thompson bought it in 1996 after seeing an advert in a grocery store magazine. It was owned by a woman who was rebuilding it in her garage after wrecking her first aircraft. They towed it to Oakdale, where Thompson – who ran an aircraft repair business at the time – put it in his shop and began restoring it. Lucas's car body shop did the metalwork on the cowl and the wheelpants.

The project took two years and included major modifications such as installing an eight-gallon auxiliary fuel tank behind the seats, and rebuilding the 65 hp Continental A65-8 engine that had replaced the original 50 hp A50 back in 1968.

Although NC21025 has no electrical system and must be hand-propped, it does sport a set of navigation lights for limited night flying. These are powered by a wind-driven generator (standard in 1938) mounted on the belly between the main gear. Another after-market modification was the replacement of the original tail skid with a more runway-friendly tailwheel.

The panel, which houses only three instruments, is dominated by a massive, centrally mounted tachometer made by Aeronca. Unlike most indicators, the needle shows an increase in rpm by moving counterclockwise from zero rather than clockwise.

With a top speed of 105 mph and cruise averaging about 90, the KCA gets a good workout. Since restoring it, Lucas and Thompson have taken turns putting more than 100 hours on it.

OPPOSITE PAGE:
The blue and yellow colour scheme is one of five Aeronca used on the KCA; it has a top speed of 105 mph and cruises at 90 – not bad for 65 hp *(CRS)*

TOP:
The KCA's stock 50 hp Continental engine was replaced by a 65 hp A-65, but since it had no electrical system, power for the navigation lights was provided by a factory-installed wind-driven generator *(CRS)*

ABOVE:
The two-place, side-by-side Aeronca KCA is 20.6 ft long and 6.5 ft tall, with a 36 ft wingspan *(CRS)*

Harlow PJC-2 (1938)

Contrary to the popular misconception, the Harlow PJC-2 was not named after the 1930s Hollywood goddess Jean Harlow. In fact, it was named after its mild-mannered, soft-spoken designer, Max B. Harlow, who in 1935 intended it as a project for his aeronautical engineering students at Pasadena Junior College in California – thus the designation PJC.

After graduating from Stanford University with a degree in aeronautical engineering, Harlow worked for a number of small aircraft companies, including Thaden, Bach and Kinner. He also served short stints with Northrop and Douglas, where he worked on the DC-2 as a stress analyst.

The prototype PJC-1 took Harlow's students only ten months to build. A group of Southern Californian investors were so impressed with the modern, all-metal design that they bankrolled its initial flight-testing and certification, with an eye to putting it into production.

After its first flight in September 1937, the PJC-1 breezed through the first half of the flight-test programme. But during spin-testing, a pilot with the Civil Aeronautics Authority crossed the controls and got the aircraft into an unrecoverable flat spin. He parachuted to safety, but the PJC-1, loaded with 400 lb of lead ballast, crashed and was destroyed.

Despite this inauspicious start, a second prototype (the PJC-2) was completed and made ready for certification testing. Perhaps because someone at the CAA felt responsible for wrecking the PJC-1, the PJC-2 was certified in a record 100 days.

Better still, the CAA ordered the first six from the Harlow Aircraft Company, which was based at Alhambra airport in Los Angeles. The newly-formed outfit was partially financed by Howard Hughes, who had hired Harlow as a consultant on the design of the record-setting Hughes Racer.

Only nine PJC-2 aircraft had been completed by 1940, when the four-place cabin design was changed to a tandem configuration in an effort to sell it to the military as a trainer. But the Harlow was not what the military wanted to fly alongside its Stearman PT-17 and Vultee BT-13, and further orders never materialised.

The years took their toll on the Harlow fleet, and by the new millennium only four examples were known to exist. The one illustrated here is the rarest of them all – the second prototype, the first PJC-2 – built in 1938 and restored by retired United Airlines captain Mel Heflinger from Redondo Beach, California.

When only 15, Heflinger talked his way into Pasadena Junior College, where he learned to fly while helping to build the Harlow he now owns. In 1961, he and two partners (who later sold their shares to Heflinger) bought it in poor condition from an owner in San Diego. They took it to Torrance airport, south of Los Angeles, and spent the next eight years restoring it. They installed a new engine, a T-shaped instrument panel and a smaller control yoke.

On 16 August 1969, after 10 000 hours of labour, Heflinger rolled the Harlow – still in olive green primer – out of the hangar for its first post-restoration flight. It has been grabbing attention at West Coast airshows and fly-ins ever since.

Only nine PJC-2 examples were built and only four remain, including one of the prototypes built in 1938 *(CRS)*

OPPOSITE PAGE:
The Harlow PJC-2 was designed by Max B. Harlow in 1935 as a project for his aeronautical engineering students at Pasadena Junior College in California *(CRS)*

N18978 was restored over an eight-year period by retired United Airlines captain Mel Heflinger, of Redondo Beach, California *(CRS)*

Cessna Bobcat (T-50) (1939)

Our featured Cessna Bobcat, built in 1944, is the beautiful yellow and black example owned by Thomas Huf of Weatherly, Pennsylvania. N41759 (serial number 5807) is powered by two Jacobs L4/R755-7 engines. Huf lives in the north-east of the U.S.A., and like many antique and warbird owners becomes a 'snow-bird' and migrates with his Bobcat during the winter months to the warmer and less corrosive climes of Florida. Huf also owned a second Bobcat, N345H (5632), which was built in 1943.

The type was perhaps intended as a competitor to the twin-engined Beech 18, which first flew in January 1937. Dwane Wallace, president of Cessna since taking over the reins from Clyde Cessna in 1936, soon had his designers working on a small, five-seat, twin-engined aircraft with a modest price tag of between $20 000 and $30 000. It was to be aimed at airlines for less busy feeder routes and as a corporate transport. The prototype was designed and built under Cessna's chief engineer Tom Salter. On 26 March 1939, with Wallace at the controls and factory manager Bill Snook in the right-hand seat, the prototype Cessna T-50 flew for the first time at Wichita.

Forty-three T-50 aircraft were sold commercially before Cessna converted to war production, under which it assumed many designations including AT-8, AT-17, JRC-1 (US Navy) and UC-78. Equally numerous were its nicknames, including *Bobcat*, *Crane*, *Bamboo Bomber* and *Rhapsody in Wood*. The T-50's role was initially as a twin and multi-engined trainer for the thousands of pilots who would have to fly the B-25, B-17 and B-24 during the war.

In 1940 the US Army ordered 33 specially-equipped versions of the T-50, the largest order in Cessna history at that time. The 225 hp Jacobs radial of the prototype was swapped for a 290 hp Lycoming R-680 and the AT-8 designation adopted. Soon after, the Royal Canadian Air Force ordered 180 T-50 aircraft to train bomber pilots, and 550 of the Crane 1-A were supplied under 'Lend-Lease' for the Commonwealth Joint Air Training Plan. Total T-50 production came to 5402. Fewer than 40 are thought to survive today in airworthy or near airworthy condition, due largely to the lack of durability of their wooden construction. Many of these are preserved in military colours as the UC-78 or Crane 1A, so it is refreshing to see Huf's civil example.

The Cessna Bobcat arrives at the April 2000 Sun 'n Fun in Florida. Thomas Huf keeps the Bobcat in the more friendly Florida climate for much of the winter, away from his colder and damper Pennsylvania home *(GPJ)*

OPPOSITE PAGE:
Thomas Huf's Cessna Bobcat has been restored in civil guise, although it started life in 1944 as a UC-78 with the US military *(GPJ*

Two Jacobs L4/R755-7 engines power this Cessna Bobcat, seen here taxying before take-off. The design had many nicknames, most common being *Bamboo Bomber*, *Crane* and *Rhapsody in Wood (GPJ)*

Bellanca 14-9L (1939)

The 1940 Bellanca 14-9L featured here is owned by Karl Ascherfeld, an 82-year-old retired USAF pilot and flight school operator from Riverside, California.

Because of its tell-tale tail fins, most people recognise it as a Bellanca, but few realise what a rare bird it is. While Bellanca 14-9 Cruisair Juniors are relatively common (44 were built), L-models powered by the 95 hp, five-cylinder Lenape LM-5 Brave engine are not. In fact, only three were built and only this one is still flying.

Ascherfeld's Bellanca is painted in the colours of its original owner, State Airlines, a short-haul regional operator that flew out of Douglas Municipal airport in Charlotte, North Carolina, and served Charleston and Columbia in South Carolina.

State ordered three 14-9Ls in 1939, but because of slow engine deliveries, it only accepted two. Ascherfeld's aircraft, originally registered NC25315 (1037), was delivered in April 1940. It was operated by State until the end of 1941. After Pearl Harbor, State's pilots, who were all army reservists, were called to active duty, effectively shutting down the airline.

In May 1943, the aircraft was sold to someone in Enid, Oklahoma, who crashed it when the engine failed on take-off. Because it sustained only minor damage, engineer Ed White (who had bought out engine manufacturer Lenape and changed its name to White Aeronautics) bought it so that he could have an aircraft powered by one of *his* engines.

Although he owned it for nearly 20 years, White somehow forgot to complete the transfer-of-ownership paperwork. He didn't realise until he sold the aircraft to Ascherfeld in November 1962.

At the time Ascherfeld was still in the air force, stationed at Turner airbase in Albany, Georgia. He stumbled on the aircraft while home on leave in Baltimore, which just happened to be where White lived too.

After flying it for a few years, Ascherfeld decided to have it restored. He flew it to a shop in Dublin, Georgia, where it was torn apart then left to sit untouched for the next three years. Frustrated at the lack of progress, Ascherfeld transported it back to his hangar in California and spent the next three years restoring it himself.

Among the extras that qualified the three-seat Bellanca as an airliner are two wing-mounted twenty-gallon fuel tanks, night/instrument-flight rated instrument panel, navigation and landing lights, and a huge heated pitot tube. Ironically, it has no flaps, and a control stick instead of a wheel.

After completing the rebuild in December 1984, Ascherfeld flew the Bellanca to many West Coast fly-ins. Although it handles well in the air, Ascherfeld says it is a handful on the ground.

It's not the Bellanca's mechanical-retracting main gear (31 turns of the handcrank raise it, 31 lower it) that is the problem, he explained; its the non-steerable tail-wheel and ineffective brakes. The 14-9L has the same 4 in, expander tube-type brakes as a Cub, which work well on a lightweight Cub but are next to useless on the much heavier Bellanca.

What makes N1KQ different from other Bellanca 14-9 Cruisair Juniors is its 95 hp, five-cylinder Lenape LM-5 Brave engine *(CRS)*

OPPOSITE PAGE:
The Cruisair Junior was 21.25 ft long and had a wingspan of 34.2 ft and the Bellanca hallmark fins on the horizontal stabilisers *(CRS)*

Only three examples of the Lenape-powered Bellanca 14-9L were built. This was the last to fly before it was placed in a museum in 1999 *(CRS)*

Howard DGA-15P (1940)

Ben O. 'Benny' Howard and his colleague Gordon Israel hit the American aviation headlines in 1935 flying his *Mr Mulligan* to success in both the Bendix and Thompson Trophy races. *Mr Mulligan*'s official designation was the DGA-6 – DGA apparently standing for Damn Good Airplane.

Commercial versions of the aircraft followed – the DGA-8 (with a 320 hp Jacobs); the DGA-9 (with a 285 hp Jacobs); the DGA-11 (with a 450 hp Pratt & Whitney) and the DGA-12 (using a 300 hp Jacobs).

They were reputed to be the fastest four-place personal aircraft on the market in 1937–38, as well as the most costly, and accounted for a total production run of 31 at the Howard Aircraft factory on West 65th Street, Chicago, near the city's municipal airport.

Derived from the DGA-11 was the heavier DGA-15P, introduced early in 1940 and powered by a 450 hp Pratt & Whitney Wasp Junior SB-R-985 engine. Forty were sold commercially before the type entered quantity production to meet military demand. The

first military order was for 250 for the US Navy, where it was designated the GH-1, GH-2 and NH-1 – the GH-2 Nightingale was to be used for ambulance evacuation duties, while others were used as personal transports and for blind-flying navigation training. Total production amounted to about 525 aircraft, and the run ended in 1944.

Larry and Terri Skinner's DGA-15P, NC52834 (717), was built in November 1943, one of the last for the military, built under contract no a(S)-1287. It was test-flown as a GH-2 air ambulance on 30 January 1944, and delivered to NAS (Naval Air Station) Chase Field at Corpus Christi in Texas on 30 May 1944. It was acquired by the Skinners about ten years ago and restored at Air Sal at Tamiami in southern Florida by Larry and Bud Skinner. Terri, Larry's wife, rib-stitched all the fabric onto the wings and tail during the restoration process. Still with its 450 hp Pratt & Whitney, the DGA-15P weighs 4500 lb gross but can still produce a 180 mph economy cruise.

Florida-based Howard DGA-15P, owned by Larry and Terri Skinner, gets airborne at Leeward air ranch at Ocala, Florida *(GPJ)*

With a superb heritage, the large, single-engined Howard DGA-15P had almost military credentials, although starting life in 1940 as a commercial aircraft for discerning civilian owners *(GPJ)*

Although 40 Howard DGA-15P examples were built for private and commercial customers before America entered the war, the majority, such as Larry and Terri Skinner's example seen here, started life as a military air ambulance designated as a Howard GH-2 *(GPJ)*

Ryan PT-20 (1940)

At a cursory glance, most observers call Dan Mairani's beautiful tandem, two-seat, polished-metal classic a Ryan STA. It's not; the STA dates from 1935 and was no longer being built when this rare Ryan PT-20 was one of only 30 produced in 1940.

The PT-20 could be said to have bridged the gap between the sleek and racy STA and the much more functional and less stylish, radial-engined, PT-22.

This is one of only two known PT-20 survivors from the batch of 30 built for the US Army Air Corps under contract AC-13316. Their serial numbers were 40-2386 to 40-2416; they were priced at $6380 each and fitted with a 125 hp Menasco C4 inline engine. They also differed from the STA in having a larger cockpit and toe brakes. A much larger USAAC order for the PT-20 was amended to the PT-21 and PT-22 which were fitted with the radial Kinner engines the corps apparently preferred. Between October and December 1940, 27 PT-20s were fitted with Kinner engines and re-designated as the PT-20A.

In the early 1970s, a PT-20A was discovered in a garage in Oakland, California, although those who saw it took it for a PT-22

because of its Kinner engine. Don Carter from San Francisco knew better and bought it. He has restored many rare classic aircraft, the most recent and ambitious project being the twelve years he lavished on a former Bolivian Air Force Curtiss Wright CW-19R working on getting it back in an airworthy condition, completed in 1999.

Carter and colleague Fred Sorenson scoured California in the 1970s for another PT-20, eventually finding both an airframe and powerplant (a Kinner, of course) in a school in Los Angeles. They took the remains of both aircraft to a workshop in the Diamond Heights district of San Francisco, where they set about restoration while searching for an inline Menasco engine. They found several being used as water pumps in Canada! Their PT-20 restoration took ten years, and in the early 1980s N14984 flew again for the first time at Schellville, north of San Francisco. Carter rarely flew the PT-20, and with the Curtiss Wright restoration nearing completion in 1999, decided to sell with only 165 post-restoration hours accumulated. Dan Mairani, a cosmetic dentist, soon became the proud new owner of the PT-20.

The rear cockpit of Dan Mairani's Ryan PT-20 with the original 1940 manufacturer's plate, stating 'Ryan Aeronautical Co., San Diego, California' just visible above the compass *(GPJ)*

OPPOSITE PAGE:
This Ryan PT-20's restoration took place in a workshop in the Diamond Heights district of San Francisco during the 1970s, before the project moved north to the airfield at Schellville for the first flight some time in the early 1980s *(GPJ)*

▲ Cosmetic dentist Dan Mairani and his girlfriend are both checked out to fly the Ryan PT-20, which is complete with wheel spats *(GPJ)*

OPPOSITE PAGE:
A neatly cowled inline 125 hp Menasco C4 engine powers Dan Mairani's Ryan PT-20, although many of the marque delivered to the USAAC were fitted with Kinner radials *(GPJ)*

With a metal fuselage and fabric-covered wings, the standard of restoration of this Ryan PT-20 looks superb in any lighting conditions *(GPJ)* ▶

Waco SRE (1940)

In 1939, while the Waco Aircraft plant in Troy, Ohio, was pumping out the UPF-7 for the civilian pilot training program, chief engineer A. Francis Arcier was busy designing a new Waco Custom Cabin. He and Waco president Clayton Brukner wanted it to be the ultimate cabin Waco. As soon as the Model E first flew in 1939, it was obvious Arcier had achieved that goal.

The first of the new Waco E series was the ARE, powered by a 330 hp Jacobs L-6 radial and certificated in February 1940. There was also the HRE, powered by a 300 hp Lycoming and certificated in November 1940.

But it was the SRE, from April 1940 and powered by a 450 hp Pratt & Whitney R-985 Wasp Junior, that became a star. In an unusual move for Waco, it was given the name *Aristocrat* in addition to the usual three-letter designation.

Its lines were a bit straighter, more utilitarian than previous cabin Wacos, but its 200 mph top speed made it hard to resist. Although it was the most expensive Custom Cabin Waco ever built, it sold well to wealthy customers.

It featured comfortable seating for four, five if you skimped on fuel and baggage. And like all Wacos, it earned a reputation for outstanding performance, ruggedness and reliability.

Despite its popularity, the SRE suffered the fatal flaw of bad timing. Had it come along a little sooner, it might have gone on to unparalleled success. However with most of Waco's capability dedicated to producing the UPF-7, only 29 of the Model E were built between 1939 and 1942. And in late 1942, when the 600-unit UPF-7 contract was finally completed, Waco got another contract, this time to build CG-4A troop gliders for the army.

It was a bitter irony that of the 13 906 CG-4A type built during the war, only 1075 were actually built by Waco: the rest were built by 16 other manufacturers, Ford Motor being the most prolific. It was, however, enough to halt production of the SRE.

With orders for more than 300 SREs in hand, Waco was anxious to resume production after the war. The last of the E-series cabin Wacos was to be the WRE, powered by a 450 hp Wright R-975-E3 engine. Although a prototype was flown, development costs were considerably higher than they had been in 1939. By June 1947 it was obvious that the bottom had fallen out of the anticipated

post-war general aviation boom, and Waco ceased trading. The last of the E-series was an HRE (NC31657, serial number 5158), delivered on 12 December 1941.

Of the 29 Waco SREs built between 1939 and 1942 only four are still flying. The most active of these is the 1941 model shown here – it belongs to Bill Nutting, 74, retired owner of a video game business from Prescott, Arizona.

The rare, straight-back Waco started out as a US Army Air Corps UC-72. When Nutting bought it in 1969 it was a basket-case, with no engine and lots of damaged or missing parts. He spent four years restoring it, adding new landing gear and building three of the four wing panels from scratch. In 1982, after nine years of uneventful flying, the aircraft got away from Nutting and ran off a runway into a ditch.

Another rebuild followed, and since then it has been all blue skies and tailwinds. N1252W had more than 900 hours on it when Nutting bought it. He has since added more than 1500 hours on hops to various West Coast airshows and fly-ins, as well as cross-country flights around the United States and Mexico.

▲
The SRE's upper wing has a span of 34.75 ft; the lower wing is 10.35 ft shorter *(CRS)*

OPPOSITE PAGE:
This 1941 Waco SRE belongs to Bill Nutting, of Prescott, Arizona, and is one of 29 built, only four of which are still flying *(CRS)*

The SRE's nine-cylinder 450 hp Pratt &
Whitney R-985 Wasp Junior at full bore
during run-up prior to take-off *(CRS)*

With a cruise speed of 175 mph, the graceful Waco SRE was one of the fastest of Waco's cabin biplane line *(CRS)*

Owner Bill Nutting shows off his Waco SRE over the rugged central Californian landscape near Santa Ynez *(CRS)*

Interstate S-1A Cadet (1941)

The Interstate Engineering Corporation of El Segundo, California, started out as a subcontractor, building components for other companies' aircraft. Anxious to benefit from the rush to train pilots, Interstate president Donald Smith decided to try his hand at building aircraft for the civilian pilot training program.

He hired Ted Woolsey, who designed the 50 hp S-1 Cadet. Although the prototype flew successfully in April 1940, test pilot Slim Kidwell recommended more power. The result was the 65 hp S-1A Cadet, which was issued a type certificate in February 1941.

By that May Cadets were rolling off the line at a rate of one a day. By the time production ceased in the spring of 1942 so that Interstate could concentrate on building L-6/S-1Bs for the military, some 300 of the S-1A had been built. They were fitted with a variety of engines, from 65 to 90 hp. Not surprisingly, the version with the 90 hp Franklin, aerodynamically-balanced rudder, and modified ailerons and elevators was considered the best of the series.

Interstate was one of many American light aircraft manufacturers that did not resume production after the second world war. The rights to the pre-war Cadet design were purchased by CallAir of Afton, Wyoming, in the early 1950s and a small number of aircraft were produced.

The beautifully restored 1941 Interstate S-1A Cadet shown here belongs to David Meeks, 48-year-old owner of an equipment rental company in Sonoma, California. He bought it in 1998 when he decided to get back into flying after a 25-year absence.

NC34939 was restored in 1993 by Tim Talen of Springfield, Oregon, a man with a reputation for turning Cadets into showpieces. He was assisted by Ron Englund, another accomplished restorer whose 1940 Aeronca 65-TL was featured in the first volume, *American Classics of the Air*.

Meeks has flown the 75 hp Cadet quite a bit since rebuilding it. While most Cadets around today are painted in the original blue and yellow factory colours, NC34939 wears an even richer scheme of forest green and Diana cream.

It's not as well known as its contemporaries – the Aeronca Chief, Piper Cub, Porterfield Collegiate, Taylorcraft BC12 – but the Cadet has enjoyed a resurgence in popularity. Of the 300-plus Cadets built between 1940 and 1942, a third are still flying.

OPPOSITE PAGE:
The Interstate Cadet is 24 ft long and has a 35.5 ft wingspan; the powerplant is a 75 hp Continental A-65, turning a wooden Sensenich propeller *(CRS)*

▲
The slab-sided Cadet is bigger than contemporaries like the Aeronca Chief, Piper Cub, Porterfield Collegiate and Taylorcraft BC12 *(CRS)*

Restoration of NC34939 in 1993 by Tim Talen of Oregon included authentic Interstate Cadet logos on the nose and tail *(CRS)*
▼

Lockheed Constellation (1943)

The Super Constellation seen here is a former US Air Force C-121C, the military version of the beloved Lockheed L-1049 airliner. It was the subject of a four-year, 10 000-man-hour restoration by volunteers of the Historical Aircraft Restoration Society in Sydney, Australia.

The Connie, registered VH-EAG and named Southern Preservation, was built by Lockheed in Burbank, California, in 1954 as a C-121C (4176). Wearing the USAF serial 54-0157, its first assignment was with a military air transport wing based at Charleston, South Carolina in October 1955.

It served in a number of USAF transport units over the next 17 years, ending up with the Pennsylvania Air National Guard in 1972. There, it served as an electronics platform until it was put in storage at Davis-Monthan airbase in Arizona in June 1977.

In April 1992 the military traded it with the HARS group for an extremely rare twin-engine Bristol Beaufighter to be displayed at the air force museum at Wright-Patterson air base in Dayton, Ohio. The transfer took place at the Pima County Air Museum outside Tucson.

In April 1993 the Connie made its first engine runs since June 1977, and in September 1994 made the short hop from Davis-Monthan to Tucson International airport. It remained there for 16 months, adding 21 flight-test hours to its logs before departing for Australia on 24 January 1996.

The first step in the restoration performed by former Qantas mechanics had been to remove the toxic pigeon-droppings. During the 15 years it had sat in storage, more than 2000 lb of the stuff had been deposited inside. The HARS mechanics had to wear custom-designed hazardous-material suits to sweep, dig and scrape it out.

With a relatively low 18 000 hours on its airframe, the Connie was in pretty good shape otherwise. The exception was the number-two engine, which HARS replaced by trading it and $12 000 in cash for one from an air force EC-121 that the nearby Pima County air museum had on display.

Over the years many instruments and parts had disappeared and had to be replaced. Tucson aviation groups helped HARS find new propeller blades, tyres and a myriad other bits and pieces.

The HARS mechanics shuttled back and forth between Australia and Tucson during the four-year restoration. Because of American immigration laws, they could work on the aircraft for only two weeks at a time.

After several false starts caused by engine problems and a leaky fuel tank, VH-EAG was ready to head off in January 1996. With a take-off weight of 125 000 lb, it was 500 lb over gross weight.

In its heyday the Super Connie could take off at 137 500 lb. But because 115/145-octane fuel is no longer available, the engines had been derated. There was just not as much horsepower available.

Although they weren't standard on the C-121, tip-tanks were installed on VH-EAG because it was restored as a civil airliner. They weren't used for the flight to Australia, however.

The crew for the 32-hour ferry flight mainly comprised retired Qantas crewmen: pilot Brian Millis, co-pilot Mike Dreyer, back-up pilots Allan Brooker and Bob Delahunty, flight engineers Warren Goodhew and Bob Hazen, and navigator/radio operator Geoff Garley of Ansett Airlines.

Also on board was Father Jeremy Flynn, the only Catholic priest in the world who flies his own de Havilland Vampire jet. He joked that he was going along to ensure a successful flight by keeping the Connie and its crew in God's good graces.

The meal service for the first leg consisted of Cheetos and Coca-Cola. Despite the distance the Connie had to fly, neither the cabin heating nor cabin pressurisation system was made operational; the crew thought the extra expense and possible maintenance problems were not worth the effort.

The Connie made an uneventful Pacific crossing to its new home in Australia. Today, it is a popular attraction at fly-ins Down Under.

OPPOSITE PAGE:
Southern Preservation was restored over a four-year period by volunteers of the Historical Aircraft Restoration Society in Sydney, Australia *(CRS)*

Often called 'the most beautiful airplane ever built', the lithe and graceful Connie is 116.2 ft long and has a wingspan of 123 ft *(CRS)*

VH-EAG turning west to begin the 32-hour ferry flight from the United States to its new home in Australia. *(CRS)*

Aeronca 7AC Champ (1944)

This faithfully restored 1946 Aeronca 7AC Champ is co-owned by Ron Franz and Rich Parker of Costa Mesa, California. Franz, 39, is the director of maintenance for Martin Aviation at John Wayne airport in Santa Ana; Parker, 50, is an accident investigator at the south-west regional office of the NTSB in Los Angeles.

According to the logs, NC83102 came off the Aeronca production line in Middletown, Ohio, on 10 April 1946 and was immediately ferried to King Aircraft Sales, an Aeronca distributor in Missoula, Montana. There it was purchased by two brothers from Plains.

In October 1946 it returned to Missoula, where Johnson Flying Service modified it as a cropduster by replacing the A65 engine with a C85 and installing a 325 lb-capacity chemical hopper in the front seat. After having its generator removed in 1950 and changing hands four times, NC83102 was sold in July 1957 to Del Monte Flying Service in Monterey, California, and converted back to a two-place trainer.

In 1960 it went to the Red Diamond Flying Club at Fort Ord; and in 1964 it was purchased by Pinkerton Aviation and moved to San Jose's Reid-Hillview airport. When Frank Pinkerton relocated to Ramona in 1966, the Champ went with him.

In 1970 it moved closer to its present home at Corona airport when two partners from Santa Ana bought it for $1000. Twelve

years later it ended up in the hands of Ron Franz's soon-to-be father-in-law, who bought it for his daughter to learn to fly in.

Although Franz's marriage didn't last, he was offered the Champ in the divorce settlement in December 1991. In 1996 the Champ had 7000 hours on it and was starting to show its age, Parker took a half interest in it, and that year they stripped it to the bone and began rebuilding from the ground up. Despite its history, NC83102 had been well cared for, so most of the parts could be reconditioned and used again. The exception was the engine, which was replaced by a 75 hp Continental A75 turning a 74 in wooden Flotorp propeller.

Because it was restored to stock condition there is no generator, which means hand-propping and carrying a handheld transceiver for communication. And rather than a glossy finish, the Champ wears the original semi-gloss coat in the factory cream and orange colour scheme.

Among the special touches Franz and Parker included are Aeronca hubcaps and tail logos and a panel-mounted fuel gauge out of a Ford A.

It took two years to put the aircraft back aloft, and since then the partners have put more than 100 hours on the Champ, bringing its total time to 7200 hours. The satisfied pilots say their Champ flies just the way it's supposed to: gentle, steady and predictable.

◀

Ron Franz and Rich Parker enjoying their Champ over the Chino Hills of southern California – green for only a month in early spring *(CRS)*

OPPOSITE PAGE:
Special touches during NC83102's 1998 restoration include original Aeronca hubcaps and a dash-mounted fuel flow gauge out of a Ford Model A car *(CRS)*

This 1946 Aeronca Champ is powered by a 75 hp Continental A75 engine turning a 72 in wood Flotorp propeller *(CRS)*

▼

Cessna 195 (1945)

Three Cessna 195s have been active in the UK in recent years, and all are shown here. Large and sturdy, they are a tiny part of the 1200 or so examples of this radial-engined type produced by Cessna between 1945 and 1954. One writer aptly described this high-wing, taildragging classic as '*a vision in metal modelling with living room comfort and a reputation as a groundlooping-Lena . . . which sets up great internal stresses among potential buyers seeking a satisfying balance between practicality and a touch of class and mystique.*'

The British-based Cessna 195B N999MH (serial number 7168) which is featured in most of these shots, is owned by London restaurateur and businessman David Ponte, who lives at East Stour in Dorset. He learned to fly in the early 1990s, converting to taildraggers while still a relatively low-hour pilot and flying with Vic Norman in a Cessna 180 at Rendcomb in the Cotswolds. He set out to buy his own Cessna 180, but found the price of good examples prohibitively high. At the same time, a Cessna 195 was being advertised for sale in Finland (under the registration OH-CSE). It had been there since 1951, and was fitted with floats. It was cheaper than a Cessna 180, and had loads more style. In 1996 he bought it, had the floats removed, and it was delivered to the UK.

Ponte finds that writer's description of the Cessna 195 totally apt. He has flown it infrequently, but realises that such a classic needs to be used. The lucky man delegated with the task of exercising N999MH is Monarch Airlines captain Nigel Barrett from Bournemouth. It was Barrett, aided by Air 2000 pilot Dean Hillier, who flew N999MH for our shoot, operating from the wet grass at delightful Compton Abbas in Dorset.

Initially called the Cessna 190, very few were built. Most of the production run was of the 195 and the military version, the LC-126. The main distinction between the models was the engine configuration. The Cessna 190 came with a 240 hp Continental radial; the basic Cessna 195 with a 300 hp Jacobs; the 195A and 195B had 245 hp and 275 hp Jacobs radials respectively. As the design developed, later models were fitted with slightly larger flaps along with a modified horizontal tail (from serial number 6084 onwards). In 1953 the Goodyear crosswind undercarriage gear was offered as standard, along with a lighter, more springy set of main gear struts. As Barrett would agree, the 195 is not the easiest of aircraft to fly, particularly for take-off or landing. Any crosswind, or a wet grass runway, makes things harder still. The big radial engine, with torque of anything up to 1300 lb of useful load, a maximum take-off weight in excess of 3300 lb, and very springy undercarriage legs, all add up to one thing – a side-slip while the main wheels are in contact with the ground can easily develop. If this isn't recognised and dealt with by the pilot, disaster could ensue. In the air, though, all the Cessna 195's attributes come into play, among them its stability, its cruise speed (around 140 kt) and its stylish and classic good looks.

The four basic models of Cessna 190 and 195 had four different engine fits. The Continental radials of the Cessna 190 were replaced by Jacobs for the three 195 models. This example has the largest, the 275 hp Jacobs, the *Shakey Jake*, along with a 50% increase in flap area compared with earlier models. Note the cylinder head speed-bumps on the cowling *(GPJ)*

OPPOSITE PAGE:
The 36 ft 2 in strutless wingspan compares with a 27 ft 4 in fuselage length. The wing chord at the wing root is almost double that at the wing tip *(GPJ)*

Appearing from behind cloud, the big Cessna 195B N999MH is not happy at lower speeds, and engine temperature soon rises. It prefers cruising at a steady 140 kt *(GPJ)*

The cockpit and instrument panel of David Ponte's Cessna 195B is largely original apart from the radios and transponder. The Cessna 195 was one of the last light aircraft, along with the Beech Bonanza, to feature a throw-over yoke *(GPJ)*

Second of the three UK-based Cessna 195 examples, G-BTBJ (6046 and former N4461C) is also based at Compton Abbas airfield in Dorset, and owned by John Griffin *(GPJ)*

Pictured close to Guernsey in the Channel Islands in October 1992, G-BSPK was the first of our three featured Cessna 195 aircraft to be imported to the UK in 1990. (Another example, G-BBYE, was sold abroad.) This aircraft was later damaged while landing at Conington. During 2000 a Cessna 190, N1551D, was imported to the UK and is now based at Old Buckenham. *(GPJ)*

Piper PA-12 Super Cruiser (1945)

Another of the many attempts to capture a slice of the post-war light aircraft market, Piper's three-seat PA-12 Super Cruiser was a reincarnation of the pre-war Piper J-4 Cub Cruiser, production of which ended in 1942. Compared with the Cessna 190/195, Beech Bonanza, and North American Navion, Piper's offering was not quite in the same category. The PA-12 was also known for a while as the Taxi-Cub: the company reckoned it would cater for travellers stepping from larger aircraft who needed transport to towns and communities not served by the airlines. Frugal operating economies were claimed – only six cents per passenger mile.

The prototype, NX41333 (serial number 5-1309) first flew in December 1945, fitted with a 100 hp Lycoming 0-235-C. By March 1947 Piper was building thirty aircraft per day, and nearly 700 of the PA-12 per month. Early in 1948, a version with a 108 hp Lycoming 0-2353-C1 was introduced. However, the writing was already on the wall for the Super Cruiser and production ceased in May 1948, with just under 3800 examples built.

The most famous Super Cruiser is still flying, preserved in airworthy condition at the Piper Aviation Museum at Lock Haven, Pennsylvania, and owned by Harry P. Mutter, chairman of the collection. This is *City of the Angels* (NX8671M), which in four months between August and December 1947 was flown around the world by George Truman, with Cliff Evans piloting sister ship NX2365M *City of Washington*.

'Earth-rounders' are now fairly common; kitplanes, homebuilt and production light aircraft now circle the globe regularly. Epic and adventurous flights, they may be, but none nearly as adventurous and significant as the journey of Truman and Evans in their PA-12 aircraft in the austere post-war years, with very little equipment to help with navigation other than a basic compass.

City of the Angels (named after its home town of Los Angeles)

and its sister ship left Teterboro, New Jersey, on 9 August 1947. The 21 countries they visited are celebrated by the national flags on the port fuselage; the 58 cities they called at during the 25 162-mile flight are remembered on the starboard fuselage. It took four months, one day – 275 hours, 25 minutes of actual flying time – for the pilots and their two PA-12 aircraft successfully to complete the odyssey, arriving back at Teterboro on 10 December 1947.

Their itinerary and their adventures are legendary. They flew via intermediate stops to Narssarssuaq in Greenland, over the North Atlantic to Iceland, Northern Ireland and on to Croydon. Then it was Cairo, Baghdad, and across West Pakistan and India. Hanoi in North Vietnam, Hong Kong and Japan were all on their route. With Anchorage they were back in United States territory. A flight down through Canada was followed by a diversion to Los Angeles for Truman and *City of the Angels*, for a hero's welcome and four days of celebration. Ten days later Truman touched down at Teterboro, with Evans about a minute behind.

City of the Angels was hailed as the 'first light-plane to circle the world'. *City of Washington* was acquired and preserved by the Smithsonian Institute. Ironically, the slightly more famous *City of the Angels* was not so well cared for, until 1997 when Harry Mutter purchased the remains. David M. Liebegott did much of the restoration work, and the aircraft was rolled out in 1998 in better condition than when it had left Piper's Lock Haven factory in 1947.

City of the Angels is not, however, some precious museum piece that is rarely flown. Mutter, at the age of 71, and Liebegott, 55, fly their PA-12 all over the United States, promoting the Piper Aviation Museum. It has flown hundreds of hours and tens of thousands of miles since its restoration. The accompanying photographs of *City of the Angels* were taken in September 1999 when it was nearly 3000 miles from home on a visit to California.

David Liebegott up-front in the Super Cruiser. Once known as the Taxi-Cub, it was Piper's hope for capturing a share of the immediate post-war light aircraft market. Between 1945 and 1948, 3800 examples were built *(GPJ)*

OPPOSITE PAGE: Beautifully restored in original 1947 colours, Harry Mutter's *City of the Angels* is preserved at the Piper Aviation Museum at Lock Haven, Pennsylvania, but is frequently flown all over the U.S.A. to promote the museum *(GPJ)*

A record of the countries and cities visited by this PA-12 on its round-the-world flight in 1947 is inscribed on the starboard fuselage *(GPJ)*

When George Truman in *City of the Angels* and Cliff Evans in *City of Washington*, another PA-12, returned to the United States after their 1947 round-the-world flight, they diverted south from Canada to Los Angeles to visit Truman's home town that had given its name to his aircraft *(GPJ)*

This Piper PA-12 Super Cruiser was restored near Piper's former factory at Lock Haven, Pennsylvania, in 1997–98 after the aircraft was acquired by Harry Mutter *(GPJ)*

Flags of the 21 countries visited by *City of the Angels* and *City of Washington* in 1947 are a colourful reminder of this historic event *(GPJ)*

Grumman G-73 Mallard (1946)

The next evolutionary step from the Goose (see page 42) and the Widgeon, the G-73 Mallard was designed by Gordon Israel and proclaimed by Grumman as 'the world's finest amphibian'. According to test pilot Fred Rowley, who flew the prototype on its maiden flight in April 1946, Grumman's opinion on the Mallard was spot on.

Although Grumman had envisioned it as a short-hop commuter airliner, most of the 59 examples built between 1947 and 1951 ended up in the hands of private companies and wealthy sportsmen. Such was the fate of N2954 (J-14), which rolled off the production line at Bethpage, Long Island, on 21 January 1947.

It was owned for a while by Howard Hughes, and later by German manufacturer Hansa Jet, before being acquired by Precision Valve of New York, which operated it for 26 years. Like most Grumman amphibians in the U.S.A., N2954 ended up in Florida – in this case, flying for Walkers Cay Air Terminal, a small commuter airline that had a Miami–Key West tourist run.

Walkers spent $250 000 refurbishing the aircraft, including full anti-corrosion treatment, two overhauled Pratt & Whitney R-1340s and fully-feathering Hamilton-Standard propellers. But in 1993 they traded up to a turbine Mallard, one of just two in existence, and N2954 went to Freeport-McMoran of New Orleans.

That's where owner Roland LaFont of Albuquerque, New Mexico, bought it in 1993. The 62-year-old US National Parks concession owner says the 1947 Mallard is his pride and joy. The first thing he did after buying it was to fly it to Ardmore, Oklahoma, to have a new interior and soundproofing installed. He also had it stripped, sealed and painted.

The following year he took it on a flying tour of Alaska. To provide his own transport from ship to shore in the event of there being no beaching ramp, LaFont can remove the last three seats in the cabin and carry a motorised dinghy.

It's just one more reason, he says, why his often-misidentified Mallard is one of the nicest aircraft he's ever flown – comfortable on cross-country flights and easy to handle on both land and sea.

The Grumman G-73 Mallard is powered by a pair of 600 hp Pratt & Whitney R-1340 Wasp H radials that burn 50 gallons an hour at the cruise *(CRS)*

OPPOSITE PAGE:
An unmistakable boat-shaped hull is the hallmark of the Mallard and the rest of the Grumman amphibian line, the Goose, Widgeon and Albatross *(CRS)*

LaFont making a low-level run over the Arizona desert between Mesa and Scottsdale *(CRS)*

The powerful but reassuring roar of the Mallard's two 600 hp Wasp radials is only a few inches away from the cockpit *(CRS)*

OPPOSITE PAGE
TOP:
The Mallard sports a gracefully tapered 66.6 ft wingspan and has a cruise speed of 180 mph, thanks to powerful engines and clean, aerodynamic lines *(CRS)*

BOTTOM:
Owner Roland LaFont, of Albuquerque, New Mexico, has owned this 1947 Mallard since 1993 *(CRS)*

North American Navion/Navion Rangemaster H (1946)

The above date, while correct for the type's maiden flight, is 25 years adrift from the date of manufacture of the Rangemaster H seen in most of our photographs. The lineage of the various Navion marques from 1946 onwards is nonetheless clear, the Rangemaster H being the ultimate development of this immediate post-war design – unless recent plans to put the type back into production materialise.

North American had perfected the manufacture of all-metal aircraft during the second world war, its ultimate achievement in the eyes of many aviators being its P-51 Mustang, many of which were built on the production line at Inglewood, California. Long before the war ended, North American was considering how it might substitute other designs for types such as the P-51 to supply peace-time markets. At Inglewood, the end result was an all-metal four-seat tourer/trainer, the NA-143, a low-wing monoplane with sliding bubble canopy, retractable nose-wheel undercarriage and fitted with a 185 hp Continental. Two prototypes were built and flown for the first time in April 1946. The aircraft did not acquire its name, Navion, until the following year.

There is no doubt that dimensionally the NA-143 was big, on a par with the radial-engined Cessna 190/195 of the same period. It was also competing with Beechcraft's V-tailed Bonanza in the private market. North American advertised its first examples for sale at between $4000 and $6200. Re-designated the NA-145, production was quickly increased and about 1100 examples of both 185 hp and 205 hp Continental-powered versions had been built by June 1947. Not surprisingly, the civil market in America became saturated as Cessna, Piper, Aeronca and Beechcraft all pushed for market share. Some earlier, surplus, civilian NA-145 aircraft were sold to the US Army as the L-17A and used for liaison work.

The older of the two featured aircraft is N8676H (see title page), a 1947 North American-built example that is owned by Doug Hoogeveen of Ora Grande, California. The engine is the 205 hp Continental E-185, standard on many of these examples. Note the many differences between this and the Navion Rangemaster H built nearly 25 years later.

North American was more concerned with military contracts

With its considerable wing dihedral evident, and tip-tanks to increase its range and endurance, the Navion Rangemaster H truly lives up to its name. It can stay airborne in an economic cruise for well over six hours (GPJ)

and its new F-86 Sabre jet fighter. On 25 June 1947 it sold production rights for the NA-145 to Ryan Aeronautical of San Diego. The Ryan Navion was almost identical to its predecessor and about 500 were built by the company, plus a batch of 163 for the US Army, which were known as the L-17B. A later, 1950, 260 hp-engined version was designated as the Navion B, of which 222 examples were built. The Navion also earned its honours as a warbird during Korea.

Ryan continued to plug its Navion for the civilian market with the Navion Utility 205, Navion Deluxe 205 and Navion Super 260. A typical Ryan Navion, flown for 500 hours a year, was said to be able to carry each of its four occupants at a mere 1.6 cents per passenger mile, flying an estimated 70000 miles in the process at cruise speeds of between 150 mph and 170 mph over ranges of more than 800 miles. However, due to lack of demand, Ryan terminated production of the type during the 1950s.

The Tulsa Manufacturing Co. (Tusco) aquired Navion's type certificate. It didn't build any new aircraft, instead modifying existing airframes by fitting the 250 hp Continental IO-470C engine. This modified type flew in 1959 and was designated as the Navion F.

It was also Tusco, which through its Navion division at Harlingen, Texas, then extensively modified the basic Navion, starting in 1961. A 260 hp Continental was fitted, along with tip-tanks, and the cockpit area was redesigned, making it a five-seater. The sliding bubble canopy was discarded in favour of access through a port-side door. One hundred and twenty-one examples were built, 101 of them as the G-1 with a modified and smaller vertical tail design. Many North American and Ryan-built Navions have been customised by specialist companies and private owners, particularly when it comes to the fitting of tip-tanks. Twin-engined versions have included the Temco D-16A and the Camair 480.

The last Tusco-built Navion was finished in 1964, and the following year all rights to the type were sold to the American Navion Society which set up the Navion Aircraft Company at Seguin in Texas. This coined the name Navion Rangemaster, and built 60 examples of the H model, fitted with a 285 hp Continental IO-520B engine. It is one of these aircraft, one of the last built, that is featured here. NAC went bankrupt in 1972 and the Navion Rangemaster Aircraft Corporation took over the design in 1974, building just one aircraft. In 1975 Consolidated Holding restarted production of the Rangemaster H, building eight aircraft, but before long the type certificate had passed to Navion Holdings of Perrysburg, Ohio, which proposed a turbocharged 350 hp Lycoming version. Several revivals have subsequently been mooted.

The featured Navion Rangemaster H, N2548T, is one of a handful of Navions based in Europe, in contrast to the United States where the type is common. It had spent most of its life in the dry desert environment of Texas, New Mexico and Arizona. It was sourced for one of its current owners, Guernsey-based Roy Greaves, by the Navion Society and Ed Kennedy of Hudson Aviation in New England.

In 1997 it was flown by its new owners across America from Texas to Vermont, where they transferred to scheduled trans-Atlantic flights. A professional ferry pilot took '48T via Greenland, Iceland, and Wick in Scotland, arriving in Guernsey on 3 October.

Everything about the Rangemaster H is large when compared with more familiar general aviation aircraft, from the cabin accommodation to its near eight-hour endurance. However, its short-field performance and low-speed handling, helped by huge barn-door-sized flaps, are just as remarkable. A recent rebuild of the wings has left this aircraft in even better condition than when originally built.

Long-range cruising at 6000 ft or more is where the Navion Rangemaster H is most at home *(GPJ)*

On the ground the Navion Rangemaster H looks a trifle gawky on its retractable, tricycle undercarriage. Tuck up the wheels and get it into the cruise, though, and with

the wing-tip fuel tanks helping, it is one of the most aesthetically pleasing and purposeful of post-war light aircraft designs *(GPJ)*

When Navion Aircraft of Harlingen, Texas, started building Navions in 1961, they made many modifications to the former North American design. The most noticeable were to the cockpit area, doing away with the sliding bubble canopy, and reducing the size and shape of the vertical fin and rudder *(GPJ)*

Cessna 140 (1946)

Cessna Aircraft Corporation's entry into the post-war light aircraft boom was the 120, a high-wing cabin monoplane with side-by-side seating for two.

The prototype made its first flight in June 1945, and less than a year later entered production. The first examples came off the line in Wichita, Kansas, in March 1946; by that August, the production rate was up to 22 a day.

With the 120's clean, rounded lines, all-metal construction, 85 hp Continental engine and $2495 price tag, Cessna had an instant winner on its hands. It was especially popular as a trainer with the FBOs (Fixed Base Operators – flight schools) that sprung up all around the country to teach veterans to fly on the G.I. Bill. (The G.I. Bill is the name of a government programme that gives money to military veterans to use for educational pursuits after they leave military service. One of the most popular uses of the money is learning to fly.) From the exposure it got there, it also found favour with the first generation of American sport pilots.

Barely a year after the 120 hit the marketplace, Cessna brought out a deluxe version called the 140. Both featured the innovative spring-steel landing gear designed by race pilot Steve Wittman; but for $500 more, the 140 offered a 12-volt battery, generator, starter, navigation and landing lights, rear cabin windows and flaps.

Although the 120 had a better payload and performance than the slightly heavier 140, pilots preferred all the extra goodies. Two years into the production run, the 140 was outselling the 120 by almost three to one.

The 140 had a lot to like: soundproofed cabin, leather upholstery, one-piece Plexiglass windshield, two tinted overhead skylights, manual four-position flaps, adjustable seats and an 80 lb-capacity baggage compartment. Wheelpants, skis and Edo floats were options, as was a $200 paint job.

Starting with 1948 models, Cessna addressed one of the 120/140's faults: a tendency to nose over with more than moderate braking. A bracket was added to the main gear extending the

The Cessna 140 has a wingspan of 32.8 ft
and cruises at 100 mph on 85 hp *(CRS)*

wheels 4 in further ahead of the centre of gravity. (This was also available as an after-sales option for earlier models.)

As the post-war flying boom petered out, Cessna made changes to the 140 in an effort to keep sales going. In June 1949 it introduced the 140A, powered by a 90 hp Continental C-90; the fabric-covered wing was now all-metal and was braced by a single strut instead of a double.

By the time production ended in April 1949, some 2172 examples of the 120 and 4909 of the 140 had been built; production of the 140A ran from 1949 to March 1951 and resulted in 525 aircraft.

Evidence of the type's enduring popularity is the number still on the FAA register: 941 C-120s, 2274 C-140s and 283 C-140A aircraft.

Jim Davis of Temecula, California, a 48-year-old area manager with the Riverside County parks department has owned this 1947 Cessna 140 for more than 20 years and plans to hang on to it indefinitely.

During the deer-hunting season, Davis uses it to help patrol the county's 16000 acres of parks and reserves in his own time and with his own dime. In two decades, he has logged about 2500 hours, raising the Cessna's total airframe time to about 3800 hours.

NC2293N is Davis's first and only aircraft. He bought the 85 hp 140 from its long-time owner in Santa Ana, California, in 1980 and bases it at Hemet-Ryan field.

He restored it after discovering severe corrosion in the wing spar carry-through and vertical stabiliser during an annual inspection in 1985. To expose the 140's skin, Davis stripped five layers of paint, some of which appeared to have been applied with a roller, he said. When he saw the shiny metal skin exposed for the first time in decades, he decided to finish it in an original Cessna scheme: bare metal with maroon trim. He also opted to paint the wings, which a previous owner had metallised in 1956. The decision paid off, because N2293N has taken first place in its class at a number of southern Californian airshows and fly-ins.

In the mountains near his Hemet airport home base, proud owner Jim Davis shows off the Cessna 140 he has owned for more than 20 years *(CRS)*

OPPOSITE PAGE
TOP:
The main wheels on late-model C-140 were moved 4 in forward with an extension bracket to avoid nose-overs *(CRS)*

BOTTOM:
Rather than polish them, Davis painted the 140's wings silver. A previous owner had metallised them in 1956 *(CRS)*

Aeronca 15AC Sedan (1947)

The 15AC Sedan was Aeronca Aircraft's first and only venture into the post-war four-place 'family flivver' (runabout) market.

Based on the company's popular Chief and Champ two-seaters, the Sedan was designed, above all else, to be affordable. Although it was an all-new design and much bigger than its predecessors, it incorporated several Chief and Champ components.

The prototype 15AC Sedan rolled out of the Aeronca factory at Middletown municipal airport, Ohio, in 1947. It received its type certificate in September 1948 and went into production later that year. Initially priced at $4795, then discounted to $4395, it was a hit with cost-conscious fliers. Besides, it was sturdy, easy to fly and maintain, and could carry a pay-load of four people, 36 gallons of fuel and 20 lb of baggage.

Some 561 Sedans were built from 1948 to March 1951, when Aeronca stopped building aircraft to concentrate on military subcontracting during the Korean war. Incredibly, more than 227 were listed on the FAA register 50 years later, including the second one built.

Of that total, 69 (including the six float-equipped S15AC) are based in Alaska, testimony to the Sedan's ruggedness and utility. Many are fitted with skis and the seats removed to maximise the cabin's 100 cu ft of space, and used as bushplanes to haul supplies to remote strips across the state.

Another reason for the Aeronca Sedan's enduring popularity is its barndoor wing. The wing spans 37.5 ft and has a 66 in chord, giving it a total lifting area of 216.4 sq ft. Add to that a fuselage that slopes down behind the cabin like an aerofoil to help create additional lift, and it's no surprise that the Sedan has an impressive short take-off and landing capability.

The Sedan also came with a choice of engines, the 145 hp Continental C-145-2 being standard. The six-cylinder Continental O-300 and Franklin 6A4-165-B3 were optional.

While it was no speed demon, the steel-tube and fabric Sedan was well liked for its solid handling and gentle stall characteristics. And its load-carrying capability made it the choice of several early aircraft endurance record-setters.

OPPOSITE PAGE:
Powered by a 145 hp Continental O-300 engine, the Aeronca Sedan has a top speed of 135 mph and cruises at 105 *(CRS)*

The four-place Sedan weighed 1150 lb empty and had a useful load of 900 lb; so with 36 gallons of fuel, passengers had to average 166 lb *(CRS)*

The 15AC Sedan, at 25.5 ft long with a wingspan of 37.5 ft, was Aeronca's four-seat follow-up to the Chief and Champ *(CRS)*

An Aeronca Sedan named *Sunkist Lady*, flown by two pilots from Fullerton, California, set a record in April 1949 by staying aloft for 1008 hours. Later that same year, a Sedan flown from Yuma, Arizona, set a new record 1124 hours aloft.

The 1949 Aeronca 15AC Sedan featured here is co-owned by Rich Heredia, 68-year-old owner of a car upholstery business in Gilroy, California, and Gilbert Garcia, 66, a retired United Airlines mechanic from Santa Clara. The Sedan had been rebuilt in October 1985 and in 1998 Heredia bought it in Arizona from the widow of its second owner. The first owner, almost 50 years before, had been a flight school in Morgantown, West Virginia.

Although it was in great shape when he bought it, Heredia couldn't resist making a few minor cosmetic changes. He installed new wing-strut fairings, tyres, bungee cords and a tailwheel, then overhauled the Continental O-300 engine, magnetos, generator and starter.

He also upgraded the radios and reupholstered the interior to match N1353H's original colour scheme, Packard blue and straw white. One of the toughest parts of the make-over was replacing the original rubber bladder fuel tanks in the wings with metal ones.

Since then he and Garcia have put more than 100 hours on their pride and joy, including trips to numerous West Coast airshows and fly-ins. They describe its flying characteristics as slow, stable and forgiving. It cruises at an economical 105–110 mph, burning an average of about seven gallons an hour, and lands at 55 mph.

Martin 404 (1950)

This rare, 45-year-old Martin 404 airliner belongs to Jeff Whitesell, 45, a Delta Air Lines captain and president of Airliners of America.

Built by Martin Aircraft in Baltimore, N40429 (serial number 14135, now registered N636X) was delivered to TWA in 1952. After only seven years in service, it was sold to California Airmotive and spent the rest of its days as an executive transport with a number of owners.

One of them was Whitesell's father, who bought the aircraft in 1973 and used it in a charter service he operated out of North Philadelphia airport. At the age of 19, Jeff Whitesell earned a type rating in the Martin and became a regular member of the flight crew.

His father had a contract with NFL (National Football League) Monday Night Football and flew the popular football commentators Howard Cosell, Don Meredith and Frank Gifford to games all over the country, Whitesell recalls. But after his father sold the aircraft, Whitesell lost track of it.

What history he has been able to piece together is that N636X flew out of Lambert Field in St Louis in the late 1970s, then spent eight years in open storage at Chino airport in California. It eventually ended up in Pueblo, Colorado, where Whitesell bought it in June 1994.

From there it was ferried to Seattle and restored over the next two years, then flown to Camarillo when Whitesell was transferred to Los Angeles. It is painted in the livery of Pacific Air Lines, a regional carrier that operated Martins out of Oakland in the early 1960s.

Pacific Air Lines was gobbled up in the merger of Pacific, Bonanza and Air West that created Hughes Airwest, which was in turn taken over by Republic, then Northwest Airlines.

Whitesell wants to commemorate these and other airlines at a planned Museum of Airline History he hopes to establish at southern California's Camarillo airport.

The crew access door is behind the cockpit, but the passenger entrance on a Martin 404 was an airstair door that lowered from the rear of the fuselage *(CRS)*

OPPOSITE PAGE:
Just as it would have looked 44 years earlier – a Pacific Air Lines Martin 404 heading north along the Pacific Coast near Santa Barbara, California *(CRS)*

An otherwise good aircraft, the Martin 404 lost out in competition against the lookalike Convair Twin series *(CRS)*

▲ The massive amount of dihedral in the 404's wing is obvious in this perfect profile view *(CRS)*

The Martin 404 was 74.6 ft long, and weighed 43 650 lb fully loaded with 1350

gallons of fuel, 50 passengers and a crew of two *(CRS)*

▼

In a manoeuvre that the 404 never would have performed in passenger service, Whitesell banks it away from the camera ship in a farewell salute *(CRS)*

Owner Jeff Whitesell testing the 404's two 2400 hp Pratt & Whitney R-2800-34 Double Wasp radials at full bore during run-up before take-off *(CRS)*

Aero Commander 520 (1952)

Its high wing and low-slung, sleek profile give it a more modern look, but the Aero Commander actually predates the Cessna 310 and Piper Apache by three and two years respectively. Its basic design was inspired by Ted Smith of Piper Aerostar fame, and the first Aero Commander, the 520, made its debut in 1952. It was quickly followed by the 560, and the most prolific of the line, the 500, in 1958. All were manufactured by Aero Commander (and later Rockwell, Gulfstream and Twin Commander) at Wiley Post airport in Bethany, Oklahoma.

The early five-seat 520s was powered by a 260 hp Lycoming GO-435-C2B engine that gave a top speed of just under 200 mph and a stall speed of 75. Because of its excellent handling, especially in short take-off and landing, the 520 is likened to flying a big, twin-engined Cessna 172.

Of the 150 model 520s built between 1952 and 1954 half are still on the FAA register; only 11 of them are older than the 1952 model (serial number 29) featured here.

Although aircraft model numbers usually get bigger as the line progresses, Aero Commander designations jump back and forth all over the place. But there's a simple explanation. With Aero Commanders, the model number was determined by the total horsepower of the engines of the particular model; the 520, for example, was powered by two 260 hp engines: 260 × 2 = 520. But like all rules, there are exceptions. The horsepower/model formula applied only to the first model in a series, not to subsequent models. While the Aero Commander 500 was powered by two 250 hp Lycoming O-540s, the 500A was powered by two 260 hp Continentals.

Barry Gregory, 54, of Moreno Valley, California, owns what may be the most spectacular Aero Commander twin in existence. Not only is his 1952 Aero Commander 520 polished to a mirror-like shine, it's gold-plated – yes, gold-plated.

N19KD didn't look anything like it does now when he bought it in August 1992. It was painted white and orange and was perhaps a six on a scale of 10, Gregory said.

A full-time metal polisher who makes his living putting a shine on cars, trucks, boats, aircraft, and anything else made of steel or aluminium, Gregory – who is known as 'The Polishing Guru' – decided to turn the Commander into a flying example of his handiwork. Two weeks after he bought it, he started stripping paint.

Once down to bare metal, he and his son Mitch began hand-sanding it in sections, one panel at a time. They started with 320-grain and worked their way through 500, 800 and 1000-grain sandpaper. Finally, the finishing touch was applied with an offset rotary grinder, and a half inch buffing pad. It took 3600 hours of polishing to get the Commander into its current pristine condition.

Since humidity, dust, salt air and even fingerprints affect the finish of bare metal, keeping it shiny is a never-ending process. Gregory buffs the aluminium with Nuvite Compound every six months and keeps the aircraft covered with a dustcloth inside a hangar.

He has added the gold-plated details one at a time over the years – more than $10 000 of 24-carat gold-plating on the spinners, window frames, door handles, nose cone, inspection panels and various interior parts. He keeps them shining with weekly applications of Pledge furniture polish on a cloth.

The Commander 520, seen low over the Temecula Hills near its home field in Riverside, California, had a 44 ft wing with plenty of dihedral *(CRS)*

Gregory has spent more than $10 000 to gold-plate the Commander's spinners, door handles, inspection panels and various interior components *(CRS)*

Powered by a pair of geared 260 hp Lycoming GO-435 engines, the Commander 520 has a cruise speed of 211 mph *(CRS)*

The Aero Commander 520 has a wide speed envelope, with a cruise speed of 211 mph and a stall speed (with flaps) of 40 mph *(CRS)*

Lake LA4-200 Buccaneer (1960)

The owner of the 1975 Lake LA4-200 Buccaneer amphibian featured here in the first four photos is Scott Janosco, a 38-year-old mobile intensive care nurse from West Covina, California.

After years of scouring the trade press and visiting airports all over the country, Janosco was unable to find an affordable Buccaneer in good condition. He finally struck lucky when he sent letters to each of the 160 owners of 1960–80 Lake amphibians registered in the U.S.A.

He got six responses. Two were too expensive, two had too much damage history and two were worth a closer look. In October 1992, he paid $46 000 for a 1975 Lake Buccaneer LA4-200 that he found in Little Rock, Arkansas. He was only the third owner of N1065L.

He ferried it home to Brackett Field in LaVerne, California in February 1993 with no heater and an outside air temperature of −14°F. The flight took 32 hours because of weather detours.

Over the next six months he restored N1065L to as-new condition, including a new interior, propeller and paint. Since finishing it, Janosco has logged more than 500 hours in the Lake and made countless water landings.

Despite its boxy, angular look, the Lake transforms itself when it takes to the air. When the gear comes up, its lines seem to stretch out and round off, making it an unexpectedly handsome aircraft.

Because it sits so close to the ground, getting aboard a Lake is easy. Open the centre-hinged clamshell canopy doors, step over the fuselage side and, using the handhold on the centre canopy brace, pull yourself in and drop on to the seat.

Thanks to the wrap-around Plexiglass panels in the canopy doors, visibility is excellent. The cockpit, which measures 41.5 in wide by 47.5 high, is a tight squeeze and reveals the Buccaneer to be a four-seater in name only.

As in most seaplanes, the throttle – an odd-looking, paddle-shaped lever – is mounted overhead. The powerplant is a pusher-configured, 200 hp Lycoming IO-360-A1B turning a two-blade, constant-speed Hartzell propeller.

Ground steering is via differential braking, but the Lake has a reassuringly solid feel as it taxies, thanks to the 11 ft-wide track of the main gear.

At full throttle, the short, stout Buccaneer (24.9 ft long, 38 ft wingspan) bounds down the runway, with plenty of rudder available to keep it tracking down the centreline. It's ready to fly at 60 mph after only a 600 ft or so ground run.

Climbing out at 65–70 mph and 500 fpm, it's obvious the Lake is no homesick angel. Most of the airframe options that the original owner installed to improve performance (gear doors, bat-wing fillets, hydro-booster hull strakes) are of mostly cosmetic value.

The only factory option that has proved to be of value are the auxiliary fuel tanks in the two wing sponsons. These hold seven gallons each and increase the Lake's fuel capacity from 40 to 54 gallons.

The gear is retracted as soon as possible after take-off, followed by flaps to 10° and power to 2500 rpm and 25 in manifold pressure. After a laborious climb to 4500 ft, you trim for level flight. Despite an advertised cruise speed of 125 mph, N1065L only does about 110–115 mph.

Both clamshell doors can be opened about half an inch, letting in just the right amount of air to counteract the greenhouse effect of the all-glass canopy.

The Buccaneer handles well in smooth air, but its relatively light weight (empty 1600 lb, gross 2600 lb) and its slab-sided fuselage and barndoor wings and tail contribute to a rough ride in even the slightest turbulence.

Because the centre of gravity is in the centre, and the 295 lb-engine is mounted on a pylon 8 ft off the ground, it creates a pendulum effect in unstable air that makes the Lake difficult to fly. For the same reason, the Lake can turn on a dime, seeming to pivot on the yaw axis.

Another unique flight characteristic is its response to power. Add power and the nose goes down, pull off power and the nose goes up. This can confuse first-timers and lead to dangerous porpoising, especially during water landings and take-offs.

With the bat-wing hull fillets, the aircraft won't stall at full power, but slowed down, a dirty stall occurs at about 45 mph, a 'clean' one at about 52. To get down in a hurry, drop gear and flaps, shove the yoke full forward, and it will descend at 4000 fpm without exceeding the 120 mph flap-extension limit.

For water landings approach speed is 80 mph, flaring to a full-stall 'plop-down' at 53–55 mph. It's important to plant the hull in the water to avoid a bounce, which can easily escalate into porpoising.

Landing 'roll' on water is about 100–150 ft maximum. Take-off run on smooth (but not glassy) water is approximately 1300 ft; after climbing onto the step, the aircraft will rotate and lift cleanly at 55–60 mph.

What started out in 1948 with the C-1 Skimmer is still going strong after all this time. Lake Aircraft of Kissimmee, Florida, got it right.

The 1975 edition of the LA4-200 weighs 1555 lb empty, 2690 lb loaded, climbs at 1000 fpm, and has a cruise speed of 150 mph *(CRS)*

Note the Lake's short retractable landing gear and pusher-configured Lycoming IO-360 engine mounted on a strut-braced pylon above the cabin *(CRS)*

Built in the 1950s, 24 Colonial C-1 Skimmers were built at Sanford, Maine. This is one of the few airworthy survivors. Its lineage (it was developed for the Lake LA-4) is obvious *(GPJ)*

A gentle taxi on the smooth waters of a Florida lake. The displacement between the cockpit sill and water has to be carefully observed *(GPJ)*

Cessna A185F Skywagon (1961)

In 1960, when the Cessna 180 was being eclipsed by the popular tricycle-gear 172 and 182, Cessna realised it would have to come up with something new to keep the tailwheel design viable. That something, in 1961, was the Cessna 185.

It turned out to be one of the world's favourite aircraft for bush and back-country flying. The aptly-named Skywagon hauls a 1400 lb payload equally well on wheels, floats or skis.

Inspired by the rugged, reliable 180, the 185 was designed as a utility craft. It was powered by a fuel-injected, 260 hp Continental IO-470-F, swinging a two-blade, constant-speed propeller.

The 185 had a useful load of 1620 lb – 6.5% more than its 1520 lb empty weight, an incredible engineering feat for its day. It had room for six adults and carried 65 gallons of fuel (84 gallon-capacity was optional).

Nearly identical to the 180, the main external difference was a deeper dorsal fin that necessitated a manual tailwheel lock as an anti-swivel device. To handle the increased payload, the baggage compartment was lengthened and the airframe, wheels and landing gear beefed up.

A belly-mounted cargo pod capable of carrying 300 lb was also available. It knocked 7–9 mph off the 175 mph cruise and 40 fpm off the climb rate, but was a popular option.

Except for minor changes, the only thing new about the C-185 when it entered its second year in production was its name: Skywagon. Other than toying with avionics, electrical systems, fuel pumps and engines, the 185A/B/C/D and A185E manufactured from 1962 to 1969 changed little from year to year.

The A185E of 1970 introduced a shorter wing and an optional cargo door on the left side of the fuselage. The 'AgCarryall' cropduster, introduced in 1972, had a wind-driven spray rig, including 151 gallon chemical tank, 30-nozzle spray booms, windshield wire cutter and vertical stabliser cable deflector.

From 1973 to 1985, when production was halted because of flagging sales, Cessna introduced a number of modifications and upgrades to the A185E/F while still managing to retain the same basic look.

As usual, Cessna has found a military role for the C-185: utility, liaison and light transport. The U17A was introduced in 1963 and manufactured in small numbers through to 1967; the U-17B, basically a standard A185E/F with Geisse castering crosswind landing gear, was produced from 1967 to 1973.

During the 24 years the 185 was in production, a total of 4427 were built – an average of 185 aircraft per year. By 1982, when our featured A185F Skywagon was built, production was winding down and only 70 were produced.

It is one of the finest Skywagons in the Los Angeles area, based at Chino airport and owned by 53-year-old retired Delta Air Lines pilot Mike Magnell, of Laguna Hills.

After flying a 185 for Foster Aviation in Nome, Alaska, 24 years earlier, he sold a Helio Courier in order to buy his own Skywagon in April 1999. He was attracted to N24579 because it was in excellent condition and was powered by a fuel-injected, 300 hp Continental IO-520 engine.

For some reason the aircraft's original Canadian buyer had never taken delivery, so it had sat on the delivery ramp in Wichita, Kansas, for almost a year. It was then sold to a newspaper in Mankato, Minnesota.

It is equipped with a factory-installed float kit, a King digital instrument-flight avionics stack, and an altitude-holding S-Tec autopilot coupled to a GPS. Magnell added an intercom and had a Snider Speed Kit installed by the Cessna Pilots Association in Santa Monica, California (primarily drag-reducing PVC thermo-plastic fairings for the brakes, landing gear legs and horizontal stabilisers).

Magnell uses the plane mainly for fun, but it is equipped with all the goodies necessary for hard instrument flying and various adventures. After all, as he says: 'That's what the 185 was built for!'

OPPOSITE PAGE:
The Skywagon is 25.7 ft long, 7.75 ft high, and has a 36 ft wingspan; it earned its name by carrying a 1765 lb useful load *(CRS)*

▶

The Skywagon is powered by a noisy, 300 hp, short-stack Continental 10-520-D turning a three-blade, constant-speed McCauley propeller *(CRS)*

The Constellation's hallmark triple-tail
silhouette *(CRS)*